THE IBERIAN AMERICANS

The Peoples of North America

THE IBERIAN AMERICANS

Sue Fagalde Lick

CHELSEA HOUSE PUBLISHERS
New York Philadelphia

On the cover: Portuguese-American children celebrating a religious feast day in Little Compton, Rhode Island.

CHELSEA HOUSE PUBLISHERS
Editor-in-Chief: Nancy Toff
Executive Editor: Remmel T. Nunn
Managing Editor: Karyn Gullen Browne
Copy Chief: Juliann Barbato
Picture Editor: Adrian G. Allen
Art Director: Maria Epes
Manufacturing Manager: Gerald Levine
Systems Manager: Rachel Vigier

The Peoples of North America
Senior Editor: Sean Dolan

Staff for THE IBERIAN AMERICANS
Copy Editor: Brian Sookram
Editorial Assistant: Gregory R. Rodríguez
Picture Research: PAR/NYC
Assistant Art Director: Loraine Machlin
Senior Designer: Noreen M. Lamb
Production Manager: Joseph Romano
Production Coordinator: Marie Claire Cebrián

First Printing
1 3 5 7 9 8 6 4 2

Library of Congress Cataloging-in-Publication Data
Lick, Sue
The Iberian Americans/Sue Lick.
p. cm.—(The Peoples of North America)
Bibliography: p.
Includes index.
Summary: Discusses the history, culture, and religion of the Iberians, factors encouraging their emigration, and their acceptance as an ethnic group in North America.
ISBN 0-87754-896-X
1. Spanish Americans—Juvenile literature. 2. Portuguese Americans—Juvenile literature. [1. Spanish Americans. 2. Portuguese Americans.] I. Title. II. Series.
E184.S7L53 1988
973'.046—dc19 87-34110
CIP AC

CONTENTS

THE PEOPLES OF NORTH AMERICA

THE IMMIGRANT EXPERIENCE
ILLEGAL ALIENS
IMMIGRANTS WHO RETURNED HOME
THE AFRO-AMERICANS
THE AMERICAN INDIANS
THE AMISH
THE ARAB AMERICANS
THE ARMENIAN AMERICANS
THE BALTIC AMERICANS
THE BULGARIAN AMERICANS
THE CARPATHO-RUSYN AMERICANS
THE CENTRAL AMERICANS
THE CHINESE AMERICANS
THE CROATIAN AMERICANS
THE CUBAN AMERICANS
THE CZECH AMERICANS
THE DANISH AMERICANS
THE DOMINICAN AMERICANS
THE DUTCH AMERICANS
THE ENGLISH AMERICANS
THE FILIPINO AMERICANS
THE FRENCH AMERICANS
THE FRENCH CANADIANS
THE GERMAN AMERICANS
THE GREEK AMERICANS
THE HAITIAN AMERICANS
THE HUNGARIAN AMERICANS
THE IBERIAN AMERICANS
THE INDO-AMERICANS
THE INDO-CHINESE AMERICANS
THE IRANIAN AMERICANS
THE IRISH AMERICANS
THE ITALIAN AMERICANS
THE JAPANESE AMERICANS
THE JEWISH AMERICANS
THE KOREAN AMERICANS
THE MEXICAN AMERICANS
THE NORWEGIAN AMERICANS
THE PACIFIC ISLANDERS
THE PEOPLES OF THE ARCTIC
THE POLISH AMERICANS
THE PUERTO RICANS
THE ROMANIAN AMERICANS
THE RUSSIAN AMERICANS
THE SCOTCH-IRISH AMERICANS
THE SCOTTISH AMERICANS
THE SERBIAN AMERICANS
THE SLOVAK AMERICANS
THE SOUTH AMERICANS
THE SWEDISH AMERICANS
THE TURKISH AMERICANS
THE UKRAINIAN AMERICANS
THE WEST INDIAN AMERICANS

CHELSEA HOUSE PUBLISHERS

A NATION OF NATIONS

Daniel Patrick Moynihan

The Constitution of the United States begins: "We the People of the United States . . ." Yet, as we know, the United States is not made up of a single group of people. It is made up of many peoples. Immigrants from Europe, Asia, Africa, and Central and South America settled in North America seeking a new life filled with opportunities unavailable in their homeland. Coming from many nations, they forged one nation and made it their own. More than 100 years ago, Walt Whitman expressed this perception of America as a melting pot: "Here is not merely a nation, but a teeming Nation of nations."

Although the ingenuity and acts of courage of these immigrants, our ancestors, shaped the North American way of life, we sometimes take their contributions for granted. This fine series, *The Peoples of North America*, examines the experiences and contributions of the immigrants and how these contributions determined the future of the United States and Canada.

Immigrants did not abandon their ethnic traditions when they reached the shores of North America. Each ethnic group had its own customs and traditions, and each brought different experiences, accomplishments, skills, values, styles of dress, and tastes in food that lingered long after its arrival. Yet this profusion of differences created a singularity, or bond, among the immigrants.

The United States and Canada are unusual in this respect. Whereas religious and ethnic differences have sparked intolerance throughout the rest of the world—from the 17th-century religious wars to the 19th-century nationalist movements in Europe to the near extermination of the Jewish people under Nazi Germany—North Americans have struggled to learn how to respect each other's differences and live in harmony.

Millions of immigrants from scores of homelands brought diversity to our continent. In a mass migration, some 12 million immigrants passed through the waiting rooms of New York's Ellis Island; thousands more came to the West Coast. At first, these immigrants were welcomed because labor was needed to meet the demands of the Industrial Age. Soon, however, the new immigrants faced the prejudice of earlier immigrants who saw them as a burden on the economy. Legislation was passed to limit immigration. The Chinese Exclusion Act of 1882 was among the first laws closing the doors to the promise of America. The Japanese were also effectively excluded by this law. In 1924, Congress set immigration quotas on a country-by-country basis.

Such prejudices might have triggered war, as they did in Europe, but North Americans chose negotiation and compromise instead. This determination to resolve differences peacefully has been the hallmark of the peoples of North America.

The remarkable ability of Americans to live together as one people was seriously threatened by the issue of slavery. It was a symptom of growing intolerance in the world. Thousands of settlers from the British Isles had arrived in the colonies as indentured servants, agreeing to work for a specified number of years on farms or as apprentices in return for passage to America and room and board. When the first Africans arrived in the then-British colonies during the 17th century, some colonists thought that they too should be treated as indentured servants. Eventually, the question of whether the Africans should be viewed as indentured, like the English, or as slaves who could be owned for life, was considered in a Maryland court. The court's calamitous decree held that blacks were slaves bound to lifelong servitude, and so were their children. America went through a time of moral examination and civil war before it finally freed African slaves and their descendants. The principle that all people are created equal had faced its greatest challenge and survived.

Yet the court ruling that set blacks apart from other races fanned flames of discrimination that burned long after slavery was abolished—and that still flicker today. The concept of racism had existed for centuries in countries throughout the world. For instance, when the Manchus conquered China in the 13th century, they decreed that Chinese and Manchus could not intermarry. To impress their superiority on the conquered Chinese, the Manchus ordered all Chinese men to wear their hair in a long braid called a queue.

By the 19th century, some intellectuals took up the banner of racism, citing Charles Darwin. Darwin's scientific studies hypothesized that highly evolved animals were dominant over other animals. Some advocates of this theory applied it to humans, asserting that certain races were more highly evolved than others and thus were superior.

This philosophy served as the basis for a new form of discrimination, not only against nonwhite people but also against various ethnic groups. Asians faced harsh discrimination and were depicted by popular 19th-century newspaper cartoonists as depraved, degenerate, and deficient in intelligence. When the Irish flooded American cities to escape the famine in Ireland, the cartoonists caricatured the typical "Paddy" (a common term for Irish immigrants) as an apelike creature with jutting jaw and sloping forehead.

By the 20th century, racism and ethnic prejudice had given rise to virulent theories of a Northern European master race. When Adolf Hitler came to power in Germany in 1933, he popularized the notion of Aryan supremacy. *Aryan*, a term referring to the Indo-European races, was applied to so-called superior physical characteristics such as blond hair, blue eyes, and delicate facial features. Anyone with darker and heavier features was considered inferior.

Buttressed by these theories, the German Nazi state from 1933 to 1945 set out to destroy European Jews, along with Poles, Russians, and other groups considered inferior. It nearly succeeded. Millions of these people were exterminated.

The tragedies brought on by ethnic and racial intolerance throughout the world demonstrate the importance of North America's efforts to create a society free of prejudice and inequality.

A relatively recent example of the New World's desire to resolve ethnic friction nonviolently is the solution the Canadians found to a conflict between two ethnic groups. A long-standing dispute as to whether Canadian culture was properly English or French resurfaced in the mid-1960s, dividing the peoples of the French-speaking Quebec Province from those of the English-speaking provinces. Relations grew tense, then bitter, then violent. The Royal Commission on Bilingualism and Biculturalism was established to study the growing crisis and to propose measures to ease the tensions. As a result of the commission's recommendations, all official documents and statements from the national government's capital at Ottawa are now issued in both French and English, and bilingual education is encouraged.

The year 1980 marked a coming of age for the United States's ethnic heritage. For the first time, the U.S. Census asked people about their ethnic background. Americans chose from more than 100 groups, including French Basque, Spanish Basque, French Canadian, Afro-American, Peruvian, Armenian, Chinese, and Japanese. The ethnic group with the largest response was English (49.6 million). More than 100 million Americans claimed ancestors from the British Isles, which includes England, Ireland, Wales, and Scotland. There were almost as many Germans (49.2 million) as English. The Irish-American population (40.2 million) was third, but the next largest ethnic group, the Afro-Americans, was a distant fourth (21 million). There was a sizable group of French ancestry (13 million), as well as of Italian (12 million). Poles, Dutch, Swedes, Norwegians, and Russians followed. These groups, and other smaller ones, represent the wondrous profusion of ethnic influences in North America.

Canada, too, has learned more about the diversity of its population. Studies conducted during the French/English conflict showed that Canadians were descended from Ukrainians, Germans, Italians, Chinese, Japanese, native Indians, and Eskimos, among others. Canada found it had no ethnic majority, although nearly half of its immigrant population had come from the British Isles. Canada, like the United States, is a land of immigrants for whom mutual tolerance is a matter of reason as well as principle.

The people of North America are the descendants of one of the greatest migrations in history. And that migration is not over. Koreans, Vietnamese, Nicaraguans, Cubans, and many others are heading for the shores of North America in large numbers. This mix of cultures shapes every aspect of our lives. To understand ourselves, we must know something about our diverse ethnic ancestry. Nothing so defines the North American nations as the motto on the Great Seal of the United States: *E Pluribus Unum*—Out of Many, One.

An artist's rendition of Spanish explorer Hernando de Soto's discovery of the Mississippi River in 1541. The Spanish were the first European settlers of America.

THE DISCOVERERS OF AMERICA

In the 15th century, Europeans first set foot on American soil. These explorers sailed the vast, largely uncharted expanse of the Atlantic Ocean, hoping to find a new route to trading centers in the Orient that would be quicker and less treacherous than their accustomed path around the southern tip of Africa. Instead, they found a New World that would become home to many of their descendants. These discoverers of America came from Iberia, a peninsula at the southwestern end of Europe that is the home of the Spanish, Basque, and Portuguese peoples.

Christopher Columbus, an Italian sailing under the flag of King Ferdinand and Queen Isabella of Spain, is traditionally credited with discovering America. In 1492, seeking a westward route to the spice-rich Indies, he landed in the islands known today as the Bahamas. In the years that followed, Columbus made several more voyages to the islands of the Caribbean and along the coast of Central America, but he died believing he had reached the Indies. Thus, the islands were named the West Indies and their peoples called "Indians."

According to Basque writer Robert Laxalt, there are those who believe that Columbus first learned that one could reach land across the western ocean from a Basque whaler who had already done so. Several Basques were members of Columbus's crew; it is possible that even Juan de la Cosa, the owner and master of the flagship *Santa María*, may have been Basque.

There are those who claim that the Portuguese reached the New World before Columbus. A map of the West Indies dated 1424 is credited to a Portuguese navigator, and others claim that a Portuguese man with the last name of Dualmo discovered America five years before Columbus. Certainly Columbus derived much of his knowledge about sailing and the sea from the Portuguese, who were at that time the most experienced navigators and sailors in Europe. Indeed, Columbus wanted to sail for Portugal, but he wound up making his discoveries in the name of the Spanish crown because King John II of Portugal refused to fund a risky trip west into unknown waters.

Despite the uncertainty over the actual discoverers of America, it is clear that all the Iberian peoples were involved in the exploration and settling of the continents

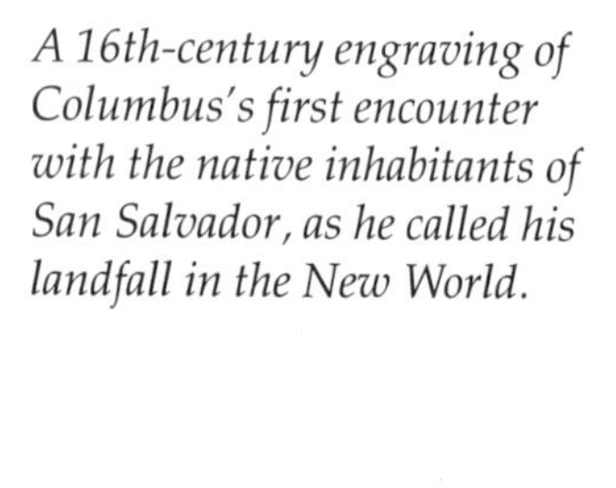

A 16th-century engraving of Columbus's first encounter with the native inhabitants of San Salvador, as he called his landfall in the New World.

of North and South America. Once the path to the New World had been established, a steady stream of explorers came to discover and claim new areas. Most of the early explorers of the New World were Spanish, but there were many Portuguese and Basque mariners and soldiers among them.

The New World

After the discovery of the West Indies, exploration of the surrounding territory followed. In 1513, Spanish explorer Juan Ponce de León, in search of the fabled "fountain of youth," discovered land to the north of Puerto Rico. He made his find on Easter Sunday, Pascua Florida in Spanish, and so named the new land Florida. He sailed up and down its east and west coasts and made a second expedition there in 1521.

Across the continent, Vasco Núñez de Balboa of Spain glimpsed the Pacific Ocean from a mountaintop on the Isthmus of Panama in 1513. Balboa's discovery necessitated a redrawing of the map of the world by European cartographers, as it was now clear that two oceans and two new continents separated Europe from the Far East. Learned Europeans were now confirmed in their suspicion that what Columbus and his Spanish and Portuguese successors had discovered was not previously undiscovered islands of the Indies but two new continents.

In the early 16th century, North and South America attracted bold adventurers from Iberia. Portuguese explorer Ferdinand Magellan, who, like Columbus, sailed for the Spanish crown, rounded the tip of South America in 1520 in his attempt to circumnavigate, or sail around, the world. When Magellan was killed in the Philippines in 1521, Sebastián de Elcano, his Basque first mate, completed the journey. De Elcano was 1 of only 18 men, out of a crew of more than 200, to survive the 3-year voyage.

In 1519, the most famous of the Spanish conquistadores, Hernán Cortés, conquered the powerful Aztec

Empire of Mexico. The Spanish then used the area as a base for further exploration in Central America and north into what is today the United States. Shortly afterward, Francisco Pizarro conquered the Incas and Peru and other areas of South America for Spain, avoiding Brazil, the land along the Atlantic coast already claimed by Portugal.

Other major Spanish explorers included Hernando de Soto, who landed in Florida in 1539 and explored the interior to the west, discovering the Mississippi River in 1540; and Francisco Vásquez de Coronado, who explored north of the Rio Grande as far as Kansas in 1540 and 1541. Members of Coronado's expedition included Hernando de Alarcón, who reached the mouth of the Colorado River, and García López de Cárdenas, who was the first European to see the Grand Canyon. In 1565, 42 years before the first permanent English settlement was established at Jamestown, Virginia, Pedro Menéndez de Avilés erected a fort at St. Augustine in Florida. Today St. Augustine proudly claims to be the oldest city in the United States.

Portuguese explorers João Côrte-Real and his sons Gaspar and Miguel are credited with much exploration in the early 16th century along the coasts of Labrador, Newfoundland, and New England. Shortly after the Côrte-Reals' exploits, their countryman Estevão Gomes charted the North American coast from Newfoundland to the present-day states of Maine, Massachusetts, Connecticut, New York, New Jersey, and Delaware.

One of the most famous Portuguese explorers was João Rodrigues Cabrilho, who was born in Portugal about the time Columbus made his first trip to America. Although the Spanish had already conquered Mexico and much of Central America, they still sought a waterway that would connect the Atlantic and Pacific oceans. While serving under the Spanish viceroy in Mexico, Cabrilho was chosen to search along the Pacific coast. After setting out with two vessels in June 1542, he reached San Diego Bay, where he went ashore and became the first European to set foot in California. He then continued northward, exploring much of the California coast before being caught in a storm that swept him past San Francisco Bay to a point near Fort Ross in northern California. In 1543, Cabrilho died of an infection that arose from a broken arm. His chief pilot, Bartolomé Ferrelo, took over the expedition and charted the entire California coast before returning to Mexico.

Settlement

Over time, the New World came to be viewed as a land of opportunity, a place where, it was said, anyone could find freedom and a chance for a better life. For young people whose lives seemed predetermined to repeat those of their parents and grandparents, lives spent in hard physical labor that offered them little hope of ever rising above the status of peasant farmer, the New World offered much more. During the 16th and 17th centuries, the Spanish settled most of South and Central America and large sections of North America, including Florida, New Mexico, Texas, Arizona, California, and other future states of the United States. They brought with them their language, religion, and way of

The focal point of a typical Spanish settlement in the American Southwest was often the open central plaza. It was usually dominated by a church, often built of adobe, or a government building. Below is a 19th-century artist's drawing of the Spanish settlement of La Mesilla, in what is now southern New Mexico.

Moving northward from Mexico, the Spanish extended their influence over most of what is now the American Southwest, including California. Here, a priest blesses the Enriquita mine at New Almaden, California, where a rich lode of mercury was discovered.

life, and they dominated the Southwest until the mid-1800s, when the United States, in its westward expansion, claimed that land as its own.

Spanish settlement in what was to become the United States took the form of military garrisons, ranches, and Catholic missions. The garrisons, or forts, were scattered along the northern boundaries of the Spanish territory to protect the land from the Indians as well as from the French and other Europeans anxious to claim it. A typical garrison was manned by about 60 soldiers, who lived in or near the adobe fortifications, launching attacks on Indians, delivering mail to nearby Spanish settlements, and serving as the frontier's police force. Spaniards who had served the crown well were rewarded with grants of land on which they carved out large ranches, called haciendas. Surrounded by the simple dwellings of the local Indians, the grand home of the landholder, or patron, became the center of a small community. The Indians worked the haciendas, tending crops, raising cattle and sheep, cooking, and cleaning the patron's home.

With the first Spanish settlements came Roman Catholic missionaries bent on converting the natives not only to Christianity but also to the Spanish way of life.

They baptized large groups of Indians into the Catholic faith and put them to work at the missions, where they learned Spanish agriculture and crafts; built dams, churches, and other buildings; cared for the orchards and vineyards; and tended the livestock. Often the missions became the centers of pueblos, or towns, that would eventually grow into modern American cities.

Although the great majority of Spanish settlers were Roman Catholic, several groups of Spanish and Portuguese Jews came to the United States seeking a home where they could worship freely. Non-Catholics had been outlawed in Spain since 1492 and were persecuted so severely that they were forced to pledge their devotion to the Catholic faith or leave the country. Many eventually settled in New York City. The oldest Jewish congregation in the United States, Shearith Israel, was founded in New York City by Portuguese Jews in 1654. Services were conducted there in Portuguese until the mid-1800s.

Most of the Spanish settlement in the New World took place in the 17th and 18th centuries. In the 19th century the Spanish colonies in Central and South America won their independence from Spain and Portugal. In North

Spanish-American women in the New Mexico village of Chamisal replaster an adobe house, a task that may be done as frequently as once a year. Chamisal is home to the descendants of some of the early Spanish settlers of North America.

The interior of a Roman Catholic church in Santa Cruz, New Mexico. Catholicism is one of the enduring legacies of the Iberian presence in North America.

America, lands colonized by Spain were gradually surrendered to the United States. Mexico, which won its independence in 1821, began encouraging both its own people and settlers from the United States to take up land grants in what is now Texas in order to defend Mexican settlements against Indian raids and to increase trade between Mexico and the United States. American settlers soon outnumbered Mexicans in Texas. When independence-minded Texans began clamoring for self-government, war with Mexico ensued. Despite their defeat at the famous Battle of the Alamo, the Texans prevailed, and in 1836, Texas declared its independence. Nine years later, it became the 28th state.

In 1846, the United States and Mexico went to war over land north of the Rio Grande that both claimed. The war ended two years later with the signing of the Treaty of Guadalupe Hidalgo, under which Mexico surrendered land that would become the states of Texas, California, Arizona, New Mexico, Nevada, Utah, and part of the state of Colorado.

The Iberian Presence

The lasting legacy of the Spanish who explored and settled much of North America can still be seen in such Spanish names of cities and states as Los Angeles, Santa Fe, Colorado, and California and in Spanish words that have become part of the American language, such as sierra, rodeo, loco, chili, and macho. Those early settlers had a profound influence on the New World, introducing such domesticated animals as horses, pigs, cattle, and sheep and cultivating such crops as sugarcane, wheat, oats, barley, and rye.

Statisticians tend to lump all Spanish-speaking peoples together, but those who have immigrated to the United States from Spain in modern times come from a country very different from those of the Spanish-speaking peoples to the south. In the 16th and 17th centuries the Spanish came to North America in large numbers.

A procession of Spanish-American Catholics in the New Mexican village of Peñasco on July 16, the feast day of Our Lady of Carmel. The women are members of a nonordained religious order dedicated to the Virgin Mary.

In the 19th and 20th centuries Spanish immigration continued at a slow but steady pace but often went unnoticed amid the larger influx of Spanish-speaking people from Latin America and former Spanish territories.

Although the Portuguese and Basques accompanied the early Spanish explorers and adventurers, these peoples generally did not settle in North America in significant numbers until much later. Both were part of the great wave of European immigration to the United States of the late 1800s and early 1900s. The first Portuguese and Basque settlers arrived on whaling ships. Others came to participate in the 1848 gold rush in California. The majority of the Portuguese and Basque immigrants came in search of a better life in North America than they had known in their homeland, where few of them had been important people. Many arrived penniless, unable to read, armed with only the name of a cousin or a godfather or a brother who might find them a job and provide them with a place to stay. But once arrived, they quickly set to work, building new homes and developing reputations as honest, hardworking people.

In the western United States, Basques became the mainstay of the sheepherding industry. A Basque shepherd might spend months alone tending herds of 1,000 or more sheep, accompanied only by his dreams—dreams of someday buying his own sheep and going into business for himself or saving up enough money to return home, buy some land, and get married. Some did go home, but many others stayed, building their homes in the same regions their ancestors had helped the Spanish explore centuries earlier.

Most Portuguese immigrants became fishermen, factory workers, dairymen, or farmers. They settled in Massachusetts and Rhode Island, where there were jobs on fishing boats and in textile factories, and in California, where many went into ranching or became dairy farmers. Large numbers of them went to Hawaii as contract laborers on sugarcane plantations.

According to U.S. Immigration and Naturalization Service figures, 250,000 Spaniards immigrated to the United States between 1820 and 1977. The largest number came between 1901 and 1930. Because they are residents of Spain and France, there are no separate immigration figures available for the Basques.

During the same period, more than 434,000 Portuguese entered the United States. Of those, 37 percent arrived after 1958, in part because a series of volcanic eruptions and earthquakes on the island of Faial, in the Portuguese Azores, forced many of its inhabitants to flee.

A Basque tends to his flock in the mountains of Nevada. Although Basque Americans still dominate the sheepherding industry, the solitary life sheepherding entails has proved less attractive to them in recent decades.

The captain and crew of the whaling boat Wanderer, *which sailed out of New Bedford, Massachusetts, during the 19th century. Because of the jobs to be had there on fishing and whaling vessels, New Bedford was a popular destination for Iberian immigrants. Most of the crew of the* Wanderer *were from the Cape Verde islands, which were controlled by Portugal until 1975.*

The number of Iberian immigrants is relatively small in comparison with the number of immigrants from other areas of Europe during the same period. For example, more than 25 million Germans and nearly 9 million Italians immigrated to the United States between 1820 and 1974. However, the Iberians constitute a significant portion of the American population, and they continue to immigrate to the United States in sizable numbers.

According to the 1980 census, the U.S. population included 177,437 people born in Portugal, 39,894 of whom had immigrated since 1975. Of the 73,735 immigrants born in Spain, 12,570 arrived after 1975. The largest number of Portuguese live in New England, especially in Massachusetts. California is home to the second-largest number of Portuguese. Many people of Spanish descent still reside in the areas first settled by Spain centuries ago. More recent Spanish immigrants are concentrated in New England and New York. The Basques can be found in Nevada, Idaho, Wyoming, California, and other western states where sheepherding has been a major occupation. Representatives of all the Iberian groups, however, have spread throughout the entire United States.

Los Reyes Católicos: The Catholic monarchs of Spain, Ferdinand and Isabella. Their marriage in 1469 joined two of Spain's most powerful medieval kingdoms and was a crucial step in the unification of the nation. The Catholic monarchs sponsored Columbus's voyages, drove the Moors from their last Spanish stronghold, and established the Spanish Inquisition.

HISTORY OF IBERIA

Until the advent of television and radio, most residents of Spain and Portugal knew little about what lay beyond the villages in which they lived. Life centered around family, church, and their work as farmers or fishermen. Few could read, and they rarely traveled far from home. They were probably not familiar with the term *Iberian*, which is used to describe people who lived on the peninsula thousands of years ago. Today *Iberian* is really a term of geography linking the Spanish, Portuguese, and Basques. Some Iberians do not come from the peninsula itself but from islands belonging to the mainland nations.

Portugal is a rectangular slice of land along the western edge of the Iberian Peninsula. In total area it is about the size of Indiana. The nation also includes the island of Madeira, located 350 miles off the coast of Morocco, and the Azores, a group of islands 800 miles west of mainland Portugal. The majority of the Portuguese immigrants to the United States have come from these nine rugged, volcanic islands, which are named Santa María, São Miguel, Terceira, Graciosa, Faial, São Jorge, Pico, Flores, and Corvo. The Cape Verde Islands, off the westernmost point of Africa, belonged to Portugal until they were granted independence in 1975. Many immigrants of mixed Portuguese and African heritage have come from Cape Verde.

To the east and north of Portugal lies Spain, which is about the size of Arizona and Utah combined. Spain occupies about 85 percent of the Iberian Peninsula. Its territory also includes the Balearic Islands, off its eastern coast in the Mediterranean Sea, and the Canary Islands, in the Atlantic Ocean.

The Pyrenees Mountains straddle Spain's northern border. Where the mountains meet the sea, in an arc along the coast, is the Basque country, most of which lies in Spain. (Approximately one-seventh of the Basque country lies in France.) Although it is not an independent nation, the inhabitants of this area have a separate and unique culture, with a language unrelated to Spanish or French and a history that dates back long before Spain and Portugal existed. The ancient Romans named them Basques, but they call themselves Euskaldunaks, which means speakers of Euskera. If you ask a Basque where he is from, he is more likely to name the region he grew up in—Vizcaya, for example—than to say France or Spain. The Basque country comprises less than 10,000 square miles and includes Labourd, Basse Navarre, and Soule in France and Navarra, Álava, Guipúzcoa, and Vizcaya in Spain.

Early Iberia

For centuries before the present nations on the Iberian Peninsula were founded, the area was subject to settlement and invasion by many different groups. The Basques, who lived in the mountainous north, were one of the first peoples to inhabit the region. One of the earliest groups to colonize the peninsula was the

Phoenicians, a seafaring people from what is now Lebanon. The Phoenicians had established a powerful maritime trading network throughout the Mediterranean region. When they founded colonies along the southern and eastern coasts of Iberia in 1100 B.C. they found native tribes already living there. The newcomers set up trading posts to take advantage of Iberia's rich mineral deposits and abundant fish and game. In the 8th and 9th centuries B.C. another Mediterranean people, the Greeks, also founded colonies in Iberia. Already well established in Sicily and southern Italy, the Greeks also saw the Iberian coast as a prime location for trading centers.

The people along the Iberian coast thus gradually became a mixture of native Iberian stock and Mediterranean colonizers. In the land's interior, however, the Iberians, including the Basques, remained isolated from the cultural influences that affected the south. At about the same time that the Greeks were founding their coastal outposts, migrating Celtic tribes from central Europe settled in the Iberian interior. Mostly herders and farmers, the Celts mixed easily with the local tribes.

In the 3rd century B.C., Iberia was invaded by the Carthaginians. These inhabitants of the Phoenician-founded city of Carthage in North Africa wished to establish military bases in Iberia from which to check the growing power of the Roman Empire. But the Romans drove the Carthaginians from their bases in Iberia during the Punic Wars of the 3rd century and in 218 B.C. began their own conquest of Iberia. It took them more than two centuries to completely subdue the Iberians. Many of the tribes in the interior, particularly in the north and west, were skilled guerrilla fighters, but in the end the superior discipline and strength of the Roman legions won out.

As a Roman province, Iberia adopted the language, administration, political and judicial systems, and culture of Rome. Indeed, the Spanish and Portuguese languages are derived from Latin, the Roman tongue, and

The crown of Recceswinth, the Visigoth ruler of Spain from 653 to 672. The Visigoths exercised power in Spain from the early 5th century until their defeat by the Moors in 711.

Roman ruins can still be seen in Iberia today. Perhaps the most crucial event of the Roman period was the advent of Christianity, which made its way to Iberia sometime in the first or second century A.D. By the 3rd century, Christian settlements were widespread throughout the region.

With the Roman Empire in decline, Germanic tribes conducted raids along its borders during the 5th century. In A.D. 412, one of these tribes, the Visigoths, invaded Iberia and established a kingdom. Another Germanic people, the Suebi, settled in the northwestern part of the peninsula. But the Visigothic kingdom suffered from internal weakness, and in the 8th century it succumbed quickly to new conquerors—the Muslims.

Empire Builders

The Muslims, or Moors as they are known in Iberian history, invaded in 711 from North Africa, where the new religion of Islam had spread from its place of origin in Arabia. Their advance halted in southern France, the Moors retreated across the Pyrenees and established their rule, called a *caliphate,* in Córdoba in south-central Iberia. The Moors dominated Iberia for eight centuries, and their legacy, especially in art and architecture, is still evident, particularly in the southern part of the peninsula.

The Hispano-Visigothic Christian lords, who had retreated to the north in the face of the Moorish advance, eventually regrouped their forces and began a long drive to oust the Moors from Iberia. La Reconquista (the Reconquest) would take several centuries and take on the nature of a nationalist as well as a religious struggle for the Iberians. These years saw the emergence of the separate nations of Portugal and Spain.

In the mid-12th century, the Portuguese wrested control of the western part of the peninsula from the Spanish, and in 1140, Alfonso I established the independent kingdom of Portugal. Spain did not emerge as a unified nation until 1469, when the two most powerful Spanish states, Aragon and Castile, were united by the marriage of Ferdinand II and Isabella I. Together they completed the Reconquest, capturing Granada, the last Moorish stronghold, in 1492. They made Catholicism the official religion, enforcing their edict through the infamous Inquisition, a royal court established in 1478. Jews and Muslims were expelled or forced to convert. King John II allowed many of the expelled Jews into his country, but five years later his successor drove them from Portugal, too.

Ferdinand and Isabella financed Columbus's 1492 voyage of discovery, but his enterprise owed a great deal to Portuguese sailing and exploration of the early 15th century. Prince Henry the Navigator founded a center in Sagres that drew the most skilled navigators and mapmakers in the land, and he sponsored many voyages of exploration. By Henry's death in 1444 the Portuguese had colonized Madeira and the Azores, discovered the Cape Verde Islands, and explored the west coast of Africa. In 1488, Bartolomeu Dias rounded the southern tip of Africa, and nine years later Vasco da Gama reached India. By the mid-18th century the Portuguese could boast of a colonial empire extending from West Africa through Persia and India to China and even Japan.

As Spain began to forge its own empire, Portugal was soon eclipsed by its neighbor. The Spanish acquisitions were primarily in the newly discovered Americas. The gold and silver found in South and Central America were sent back to Spain, and the Spanish crown, which held trade monopolies in its colonies, became rich and powerful. Up to the late 16th century, Spain ruled the seas and was the most powerful nation in Europe, with an empire

A late-15th-century engraving of the harbor of Lisbon, Portugal's most important city, by Theodore DeBry. In the 1400s, the voyages sponsored by Prince Henry the Navigator and other Portuguese monarchs made Portugal one of the world's most important seafaring and commercial powers.

that included a large section of the Western Hemisphere and portions of Africa and Asia. As Spain grew in power, a weakened Portugal came under its control, and in 1580, under King Philip II, Spain occupied its neighbor.

Spain's power and influence began to wane with the defeat of the Spanish Armada by English naval forces in 1588. Consisting of 130 ships and 30,000 men, the Armada was assembled by the king of Spain, Philip II, to invade England.

At the same time, other European nations were beginning to challenge Spain's control of the seas and trade monopolies. Trying to exert its new power to influence European politics, Spain became embroiled in continuous wars that drained its wealth. The loss of Spanish control of the seas was dramatically illustrated in 1588, when the mighty Spanish Armada, the pride of King Philip II's forces, was destroyed by the English. Spain then began a long period of decline, weakened by internal strife and the drain on its resources caused by war and the upkeep of its colonies. However, at the same time, Spain's arts flourished. It was during this period that the great artists El Greco, Bartolomé Murillo, and

Diego Velázquez painted their masterpieces and Miguel de Cervantes wrote his seminal novel, *Don Quixote*.

Under John IV, of the Bragança dynasty, Portugal regained its independence in 1640, but its overseas empire was beginning to erode. The Dutch wrested away control of the valuable spice trade with the East Indies, and the English and Dutch both challenged Portugal's monopolies in the Far East. But with the discovery of gold and diamonds in the Portuguese colony of Brazil during the reign of John V, Portugal enjoyed a cultural renaissance and renewed prosperity.

Although not a Spaniard by birth, the painter El Greco raised Spanish art to new heights in the late 16th century. Reproduced here is his greatest masterpiece, The Entombment of Count Orgaz.

The Growth of Republics

Like the rest of Europe, Spain and Portugal were greatly affected by the upheaval caused by the French Revolution and the rise of Napoléon Bonaparte in the late 18th century. In an effort to contain the Revolution, both countries allied themselves with England. When Portugal was threatened with invasion by Napoléon's army, its royal family fled to Brazil, but its English allies continued the fight against Napoléon on Portuguese soil, causing great destruction. Napoléon also invaded Spain in 1809 in an attempt to force the Spanish to accept his brother, Joseph Bonaparte, as their new king.

In 1815, Napoléon was defeated at the Battle of Waterloo and was sent into exile, but the effects of the French Revolution and the Napoleonic Wars were enduring. The French revolutionary ideals of liberty, equality, and fraternity combined with discontent with the ruling monarchies to inspire movements toward constitutional and representative governments. In Spain, monarchists and republicans battled in a series of armed struggles, known as the Carlist Wars, that began in 1833 and continued intermittently for the rest of the century. These wars left the Spanish people with a deep distrust of civilian government, and military figures began to emerge as political leaders.

This portrait of Philip III, king of Spain and Portugal, helped Diego Velázquez win the monarch's approval. Under Philip's patronage, Velázquez created the works that have won him a lasting reputation as one of the greatest of all European painters.

Throughout the 19th century, Spain and Portugal gradually lost many of their overseas possessions. The loss of Brazil in 1822 dealt the Portuguese economy a crippling blow, as it had depended on income from Brazil's precious stones and metals. Spain was stripped of its last colonies in the Americas—Cuba and Puerto Rico—as well as the Philippines during the Spanish-American War of 1898. The humiliatingly quick defeat at the hands of the Americans produced a sudden malaise among the Spanish, who called the loss "the Disaster."

In Portugal the republican movement steadily grew in strength until 1910, when King Manoel II was driven

The Executions of the Third of May *by Francisco de Goya depicts French troops shooting Spanish patriots opposed to the rule of Napoléon Bonaparte. In Spain, Napoléon was initially welcomed as a champion of democracy, but his imperial ambitions ultimately alienated the Spanish, who came to revile him as a foreign interloper.*

out and a republic was declared. But the republicans were divided internally and were themselves overthrown in a military coup led by General Antonio de Carmona in 1926. Carmona remained president until 1951, but the real ruler of Portugal was his finance minister, Antonio de Oliveira Salazar. Determined to drag Portugal into the modern era, Salazar proclaimed the formation of an Estado Novo—New State—and established a national assembly, enacted development plans, and promoted industrialization. He quickly and ruthlessly stifled any opposition, ruling as a virtual dictator until his death in 1970. The constitutional movement continued to grow in Spain. In 1923, General Miguel Primo de Rivera staged a coup that overthrew the discredited monarchy. But the republic he established was plagued by division and unrest, and in July 1936, Francisco Franco led a conservative military uprising, backed by the Spanish Fascist party, the Falange. Aided by Adolf Hitler's Nazi Germany and Benito Mussolini's Fascist Italy, Franco conducted a bloody 3-year war that led to the death or emigration of 1 million Spaniards, including many leading intellectuals. In part because of the enormous physical destruction caused by the war, the Spanish suffered many years of hardship under Franco, who ruled as dictator until 1975. Upon his death, under an agreement made in 1969, Prince Juan Carlos de Borbón became the head of state as king of Spain.

Portugal suffered a political crisis in the early 1970s over the issue of decolonization. One of the few countries of the world that still possessed colonies, Portugal suffered from political isolation over its refusal to free its subjects and from the economic drain of maintaining the colonies. In 1974, General Antonio de Spinola came to power in a military coup; a Marxist faction soon gained control of the government and in 1975 granted independence to Portugal's African colonies: Guinea-Bissau, Angola, and Mozambique. Thousands of colonial refugees poured into Portugal, putting an enormous strain on the economy, but they gradually and peacefully assimilated into Portuguese society.

A beaming Francisco Franco (right) welcomes Nazi dictator Adolf Hitler (left) to Spain in November 1940. The previous year Franco had forced the surrender of the Loyalists, his opponents in the Spanish civil war, and established himself as Spain's dictator.

Under Juan Carlos, Spain has moved toward a more democratic form of government, with legal political parties and elected officials. A democratic constitution was put into effect in 1978, and Spain is now a constitutional monarchy, with an elected legislature, the king as head of state, and the prime minister as the head of government. After its 1974 revolution, Portugal, too, slowly returned to republican government. The free elections held in Portugal since 1976 have demonstrated the success of this transition. Both Spain and Portugal belong to the European Community, although they are among its poorer members. Both play an active role in European politics and plan to be part of the proposed economic unification of Europe, scheduled to take place by 1992.

The Basques

Basque history is in many ways the history of Spain and France, but despite their ties to these two nations, the

Hand placed on Bible, Juan Carlos de Borbón is sworn in as the first king of the restored Spanish monarchy on November 22, 1975, two days after the death of Franco.

Basques have maintained a separate identity. Historians are not sure of the origin of the Basques, but they generally agree that they are the oldest identifiable ethnic group surviving in western Europe. Their language, which cannot be traced to any other spoken or written tongue, sets them apart, as does a curious biological fact: There are practically no Basques with type-B blood, but Basques have the highest incidence of type O and of the Rh-negative factor of any people in the world.

Early Basques were hunters who gradually turned to farming in the inland areas and fishing along the coasts. They resisted invasions of the peninsula by the Romans, Visigoths, and Moors with an effective form of guerrilla warfare. However, the Basques, a fiercely independent people, remained a confederation of tribes, uniting only to fight common enemies but never forming a separate country with a central government.

When Spain and France established control over the Basque territory, it did not at first affect the Basque way of life. The governments of those countries promised to respect the rights and customs already established, but over the years those promises have often been broken.

During the French Revolution, French Basques opposed the policies of the new government, and many lost their land and livestock and were imprisoned. During Napoléon's campaigns, both the French and Spanish armies left a trail of bloodshed and property damage in the Basque country.

Spanish Basques were caught up in several other wars. In 1833 and 1839, they were on the losing side of the Carlist Wars, and their long-held rights began to disappear. They were heavily taxed, their men were drafted into the military, and when the Carlists were defeated, they were left with heavy war debts.

After Franco emerged victorious in the Spanish civil war, he punished the Basques for siding with the opposition. For nearly 40 years, until a new Spanish constitu-

At a press conference in Bordeaux, France, four hooded Basque terrorists take responsibility for the bomb blast that claimed the life of Spain's prime minister, Luis Carrero Blanco, in December 1973. The Basque separatist movement has waged a long, sometimes violent campaign for independence.

tion was approved in 1978, he prohibited use of the Basque language or participation in Basque cultural events. As a result, today there are sections of the Basque country where Spanish is spoken instead of Basque. After Franco's death, the Spanish Basque region was granted the right to rule itself, and a parliament was elected in 1980. However, many Basques still yearn for complete independence.

The Decision to Emigrate

The frequent tumult on the Iberian Peninsula was an important factor in the decision of many Iberians to leave their homeland and start life in a new country.

In Portugal, when a young man turned 16, he was required to serve 8 years in the military. For many, especially those in the Azores, who felt little connection with the government of the mainland, this seemed an unfair burden. The wealthy commonly hired substitutes to serve for them, but poorer families could not afford to do this, and many smuggled their sons aboard ships and sent them to America instead.

The Basques likewise were not eager to serve in the military of either Spain or France, and many escaped across the borders or immigrated to America. More than half of the young men in some villages left during the late 1800s in order to escape the draft. Many young Spaniards also decided to seek their fortune elsewhere rather than serve in the army.

In addition to suffering the consequences of their countries' wars and wanting to escape military service, many Iberians left home because of the poverty that always seemed to be a part of their life.

In the Azores, for example, there is little room for planting crops. Early farmers tried a wide variety of crops, many of which failed, including citrus fruits, tobacco, sugarcane, wheat, and flax. Others, such as potatoes, beans, corn, and wine grapes, became staples for the Azorean farmers, who grew as much as they could

The checkerboard landscape of the island of Terceira, in the Azores. The small landholdings of much of the rural populace of the Azores leave it susceptible to economic downturns and natural disasters.

on their small plots of land but still had barely enough for their families.

Agriculture was also the main occupation of most of the Basques as well as of the majority of the Spanish and the Portuguese. In the 1800s, Iberian farmers still used traditional, primitive agricultural methods and depended on nature for the success of their crops. They often faced years of great hardship. A famine ravaged the Basque country in 1846–47. In Portugal in 1850, potato rot swept through the fields, grapevines were attacked by disease, crippling wine production, and a parasite destroyed the citrus crops. In other years, there were wars, windstorms, droughts, or other disasters to wreak havoc on crops.

Unequal distribution of land only made matters worse. In Portugal, a small number of wealthy people owned all the land, leasing portions to tenant farmers, who paid their rent either in crops after the harvest or in cash at the end of the year. Even in years when the crops failed, the rent stayed the same, so the farmers were always in debt, with no hope of ever owning their own land. The leases could be passed down to their children, but large families were common, and the farms were too small to be shared by all. In the 19th century in the Azores, where land was exceedingly scarce, the population grew to the point where hunger was commonplace. In Spain also, land was held by a small group of wealthy people who rented it out in small portions to peasant farmers.

The Basque system of land ownership was somewhat different. Individual families owned the land, passing it on intact to the next generation. However, only one child in each family was designated as the one who would inherit his parents' land. Since arable land in the mountainous Basque country was scarce, the other children were provided with cash dowries and were expected to make their living in some other way, either by marrying someone who had inherited land, finding a new occupation, or immigrating to the New World.

Family and God First

Life in Iberian villages seldom changed from generation to generation, and people spent their entire existence in the village in which they were born. Everyone knew and helped each other. Families worked together, and there existed an extensive network of siblings, cousins, and godparents who could be relied on for help. One's role in life was determined long before birth. As Jerry Williams wrote in *And Yet They Come*, there were few identity crises in Iberian villages: Within the family, the father was the boss, women played a subordinate role, and children were expected to obey without question.

In the Basque country, each household provided for itself, raising cows, pigs, chickens, and sheep and growing corn, wheat, apples, and other crops to live on. The villagers shared a common central area in which livestock could graze. They needed little money, and most commerce took the form of bartering for goods. Extra cash was earned by selling livestock or taking seasonal jobs as loggers during the winter. Children from large families were sometimes loaned out to neighboring families, living with them and helping them work their farms.

Life in the Iberian villages revolved around the church. Nearly all of the Portuguese, Spanish, and Basques were Roman Catholic, and their lives were governed by the rules and rituals of the church, combined with long-held folk beliefs and myths. In Portugal, for example, many believed in the "evil eye," the power of certain people to cast a spell by looking at someone. Most villages had no hospitals and treated illness with prayer and magic. Religious holidays were occasions for processions and celebrations by the whole village.

The church was the main source of education for most Iberians. While there were schools here and there, attendance was not enforced, and many families kept their children home to work. Most peasants believed that only kings, government officials, priests, and merchants needed to know how to read. "The average farm laborer or fisherman did not see much value in a formal education," wrote Leo Pap, author of *The Portuguese Americans*. "One did not have to read to know what was going on in the village. Why should children waste years in school when they could help on the farm instead?"

Illiterate, poor, bound by centuries of tradition, most Iberians led difficult lives. It is little wonder, then, that when their countrymen who had left for America sent back glowing reports from the New World, many considered journeying there themselves.

The Spanish earth: A Spanish peasant enjoys a moment's rest from his labor.

The crew of the whaling ship Sunbeam *(photographed circa 1900) was composed of immigrants from mainland Portugal and the Cape Verde Islands.*

IBERIANS COME TO AMERICA

When an Iberian emigrant stepped on board a ship bound for America, he never knew for certain if his feet would touch home ground again. He had heard so much about America but had little real idea of what it would be like. Reaching into his pocket for a slip of paper, he reread the name of his cousin and the town where he lived: Gloucester, a word he could not begin to pronounce. He turned his gaze skyward and whispered a prayer to God for his safety.

With him on the ship were many others bound for the New World. Most spoke Portuguese or Spanish and were young men like himself who planned to send for their families or their sweethearts as soon as they had enough money and a place for them to live. Some had jobs waiting for them, working with a relative on a farm or in a factory, on a sheep ranch or a sugar plantation. Others did not know what they would do upon arrival. They came for many reasons. Some were farmers who could not get land of their own at home but had heard that in America land stretched as far as the eye could see. Others were weary of so much hard work with so little

Antonio Mandly was born on the island of Graciosa, in the Azores, but as a young man he made his way to New Bedford, where he won fame as a whaling captain. Between 1885 and 1925 he commanded 28 whaling expeditions.

reward and believed America offered them the opportunity to do better. Many were tired of wars and revolutions and of taking orders from government officials. Some were young men who had slipped away from their villages at night to stow away on passenger ships or whaling ships in order to avoid military service.

A few were driven to cross the sea by the prospect of finding a place where they could freely practice their religion. A colony of Jews had gone to America in the 1600s and established synagogues in New York and Rhode Island. By 1863 there were 2,000–3,000 Iberian Jews in the United States. In the 1850s a congregation of Portuguese Protestants made homes for themselves in Illinois, where the area they settled is still known as Portuguese Hill. There were many reasons to leave Iberia for America, but most immigrants simply hoped for a chance for a better life.

Whalers and Draft Dodgers

The first large group of immigrants from Iberia, many of whom were from the Azores, came on whaling ships in the late 1800s. Based in New Bedford, Massachusetts, and other New England ports, the ships would customarily stop in the Azores for fuel and supplies before heading around the world in search of the whales that provided the oil used in soaps, medicines, and fuel. Often they would pick up some Azorean crew members, especially as American sailors wearied of the long journeys and low pay. With their home islands providing less economic opportunity with each passing year, the Azoreans eagerly stepped in as replacements, often not realizing what they were getting into.

Many of the captains of the whaling vessels were heartless men who worked their crews mercilessly, denying them the proper measure of sleep and food. Some punished their men severely for the slightest mistake, and many looked down on the dark-skinned Azoreans and Cape Verdians. "Descriptions are found in diaries kept by these poor Azorean souls who found themselves many a time serving the devil rather than a human being, whose promises of quick travel to American shores would only materialize one or two years later, if at all," Carlos Almeida wrote in *The Portuguese Immigrants.* The men were not always given accurate information about when the trip would end, and in many cases they had reason to doubt whether they would be paid fairly when it was over. On most whaling ships, no wages were offered. The sailors instead received a share of the profits from the oil after the captain's larger portion and fees for clothing, food, and other supplies were deducted.

Two Azorean children pose in the rubble of their home village of Horta, on the island of Faial, following an earthquake there in 1897. Earthquakes, volcanic eruptions, and other natural disasters combined with poverty to convince many Azoreans to emigrate to the United States.

The whaling ships were often gone for two or more years. Life on board was tough, but many Azoreans and others from Iberia were eager to sign on because it offered a chance to get to America. Although most of the whalers landed in New England, some brought immigrants to Hawaii or California. During the California gold rush, crew members, eager to prospect for the precious metal, often jumped ship, swimming ashore under the musket fire of their angry captain.

Many young Azoreans with no sailing experience chose to stow away on merchant ships or passenger liners. Large numbers were smuggled aboard by their parents, who paid their passage and a fee to an agent who arranged the trip.

No matter what method they chose, young Portuguese men who left home had to do so surreptitiously if they had not fulfilled their military obligation or paid someone to serve for them. The Spanish also often left their homeland illegally. In the early 1900s, Spain forbade its citizens to emigrate, but between 1906 and 1913, 8,000 Spanish were imported to work on the sugar plantations in Hawaii. Many were smuggled out from Gibraltar. Some stayed for a while in Chile, Cuba, Mexico, or Puerto Rico before heading north. Although the Spanish government tried to restrict migration to the Americas by requiring licenses and fees, violation of the rules was flagrant.

Basques from both the French and Spanish sectors slipped across the border to avoid the draft. The French Basques, who made up only a small portion of the total French population, accounted for nearly half the draft evaders in that country. Although 19 year olds in France could not hold passports, they crossed the border into Spain and left from Spanish ports. Boats leaving with loads of legal emigrants would stop to pick up the illegals at Pasajes before crossing the Atlantic. Spanish Basques crossed into France and departed from Bayonne, Bordeaux, and other ports.

Mass Migration

The largest number of Iberian immigrants came to North America in the early decades of the 20th century, which was also the high point of European immigration. Although U.S. immigration statistics do not record the large numbers of undocumented Iberian immigrants who entered the country, they do provide an indication of the comparative volume of immigration at different periods. Records show that between 1820 and 1900 about 42,000 Spaniards immigrated to the United States, but that number increased to 100,000 between 1901 and 1931. Between 1820 and 1974, 243,761 Spanish and 389,845 Portuguese immigrated to the United States. Spanish immigration reached its height during World War I, when unskilled Spanish newcomers found jobs in eastern munition plants and shipyards and miners from the Spanish province of Asturias went to work in West Virginia coalfields. The largest number of Portuguese came during the first part of the century, when they were able to find jobs in the cotton mills of New England.

As methods of transportation improved, more immigrants came to the United States. The early immigrants who did not choose to board a whaling ship made the passage across the Atlantic on cargo and passenger ships. These sailing ships were often uncomfort-

Loaded to the gunwales with Cape Verdian immigrants, the Savoia *arrives at New Bedford, circa 1900.*

able and slow, taking one to three months to make the journey. The advent of the steamship made the trip much easier. In 1902, the American White Star Line established twice-a-month steamer service to the Azores. Six years later, the Fabre Line set up a direct route from the Azores to Providence, Rhode Island. Until 1920, Providence was the most likely place of arrival for Azoreans coming to America. Other shipping lines also developed regular transatlantic service.

The steamships cut travel time down to 10 days or less, and because they were built to carry passengers, they had better accommodations than the sailing ships. Lodging in steerage—the section occupied by passengers paying the lowest fare—although still dark, stuffy, and often overcrowded, nevertheless represented an improvement over the sailing ships.

Nearly all of the first immigrants were men, but women and children began leaving Iberia in significant numbers in the early 1900s. From 1900 to 1919, the ratio of men to women was still three to two, though there were no restrictions on women leaving Spain or Portugal. Over the years, the numbers gradually balanced out.

Family members and friends sent back letters praising America in glowing terms and urging their countrymen to join them. In many villages in the Basque country, for example, most families had at least one relative in the New World. Thus, a significant percentage of the immigrants came to rejoin family or friends already in America. In 1890, one-quarter to one-third of the Iberian immigrants traveled to North America on

Paquetes a' Velad e New Bedford.

Carreira dos

AÇORES e MADEIRA

A muito conhecida e veleira barca

"VERONICA,"

Capitao NARCIZO DE AZEVEDO,

Sahirá do porto de New Bedford, aproximadamente, no dia

15 de Maio proximo.

Para a MADEIRA, tocando nas ilhas das FLORES, FAYAL, S. JORGE, TERCEIRA e S. MIGUEL.

Esta barca foi construida expressamente para a carreira dos Açores, e tem todas as condiçoes e commodidades necessarias para o conforto dos passageiros, dando-lhes sempre a maior garantia de bom tratamento.

A "Veronica" faz as mais breves viagens que se teem feito e pódem fazer entre a America e Açores.

Para passageiros, fretes e mais informaçoes trata-se com os consignatarios, que sao:

Nas FLORES—James Mackey; no FAYAL—Bensàude & Co.; em S. JORGE—Joaquim Jose Cardozo (Vélas) e Francisco Machado d'Avila (Ribeira Secca); em S. Miguel—Domingos Dias Machado; e em NEW BEDFORD os proprietarios, Loum Snow & Son, 29 North Front street, e Antonio L. Sylvia, 159 South Water street.

Acha-se constantemente na agencia dos proprietarios um bom sortimento das melhores e mais puras qualidades de vinho do Porto e Madeira.

Vendem-se ali bilhetes de passagens em todas as estradas de ferro para a California e todos os pontos no Oeste.

Promptificam-se a remetter dinheiro e mercadorias de qualquer genero para qualquèr das

This advertisement for passage between New Bedford and the Azores appeared in 1885 in Progresso Californiense, *a Portuguese-language newspaper published in San Francisco in 1885. At the time, travelers to or from the Azores had to meet their ships or disembark at ports on the East Coast of the United States.*

prepaid tickets. In 1901, the U.S. Industrial Commission found that approximately half came on prepaid tickets or paid their fares with money sent by relatives already living in the United States.

With the increased interest in immigrating, shipping companies began to advertise and offer extras to entice prospective immigrants into using their ships. In 1911, the Venezia Line advertised monthly service between Terceira and the United States, promising arrival in five and a half days and providing transportation from the East Coast to California on the fastest railroad available.

But even at reduced rates, the cost of a steamship ticket represented a significant investment for many Iberian families. In 1902, steamship passage from Ponta Delgada, Faial, to the United States cost $23, but many of the immigrants who made the journey could barely afford it. Some arrived penniless after having spent all their money on the fare. Others borrowed the money and repaid it after they found work in America.

First Steps

Upon arrival in the United States, the immigrants joined thousands of other Europeans as they went through a series of medical tests and answered questions about their history, education, and financial status. Some were sent back home because they were sick, showed signs of insanity or unacceptable morals, had committed crimes, or seemed to have no way to support themselves. Many were detained until a friend or relative showed up to vouch for them. Women traveling alone were not released until a male took responsibility for them.

Most immigrants who came to the United States between 1855 and 1890 were processed at the Castle Garden immigration center, at the southern tip of Manhattan in New York. In 1892, nearby Ellis Island became the main immigrant receiving station. Its procedures were copied at receiving stations in other eastern ports, including Providence, Rhode Island, where most Portuguese debarked. In some cases, families were separated because a husband, wife, or child was deemed unacceptable and sent home. While most immigrants were admitted, they regarded immigration officials with great fear and sometimes had to wait several days to be processed.

Those who had family or friends waiting for them met them and went on. Others had their destination printed on a card pinned to their shirt and were directed to trains bound, they hoped, for where they planned to go. For many Basques, the first stop was a Basque hotel run by a countryman who could point them toward jobs and transportation.

In the 19th century, European immigrants were accepted, if not always welcomed, because the U.S. economy needed the labor they provided. In the 20th century, however, people began to worry that the seemingly unending flood of European immigrants would deprive Americans of jobs and wash away the American way of life. As a result, a series of laws were passed that severely restricted the number of Iberian (and other European) immigrants allowed to enter.

The Portuguese were particularly hard hit by legislation enacted in 1917 that required immigrants over the age of 16 to pass a literacy test. At the time, only about 30 percent of the Portuguese population could read. Only three years of education were required, and many Portuguese did not attend school at all. The mandatory education requirement was raised to six years in the 1960s, but the illiteracy rate in Portugal is still among the highest in Europe. Although the reading tests given by immigration officials were not difficult—the immigrants were given 30 to 40 words in their own language to read—most were still unable to pass them, and the number of Portuguese immigrants admitted dropped dramatically. The only ones allowed to enter without passing the test were those who had come to join their family.

Basques relax with a game of cards at a Basque hotel in Mountain Home, Idaho. Because so many Basque immigrants earned a living from rural occupations that left them geographically isolated, Basque hotels served them as restaurants, clubhouses, social centers, information clearinghouses, and mail drops.

The literacy requirement, which remained in effect until 1952, did not pose as large an obstacle for the Spanish. Most of the immigrants from Spain were better off financially, and 85 percent of those over the age of 14 knew how to read. Many were also skilled in various trades.

However, all would-be Iberian immigrants were affected in 1921 by the imposition of the first immigration quotas, which limited the number of people admitted from each country annually to 3 percent of the number of people of that nationality living in the United States in 1910. The number was revised to 2 percent in 1924 and lowered again in 1927. Initially, only 912 Spaniards per year were allowed to enter the United States; that number was later reduced to 131, including Basques. The quota for Portuguese immigrants was set at 520 in 1921, then lowered to 503 in 1924 and 440 by 1929. The only exceptions to the quotas were the children and spouses of American citizens, previous immigrants who were returning, and immigrants from other countries in the Western Hemisphere. Many Iberians went to South America and then made their way to the United States in order to circumvent the quotas.

The quotas remained in place until 1965, when President Lyndon Johnson signed the U.S. Immigration and Nationality Amendments Act, which allowed entry to 20,000 immigrants per year from each independent country outside the Western Hemisphere and to 120,000 immigrants from within the Western Hemisphere.

Even when the quotas were in effect, exceptions were made for economic or humanitarian reasons; for example, when the need for more Basque sheepherders became apparent in the 1940s and when the Azores were struck by a series of volcanic eruptions and earthquakes in the late 1950s, special legislation was enacted to allow more immigrants to enter the country. Despite these measures, the number of Iberian immigrants in a given year never equaled its pre-1921 peak.

The textile mills of Lowell, Massachusetts, attracted many Iberian, French-Canadian, and Italian immigrants. These Portuguese-American mill workers were photographed in Lowell in 1912.

In recent years, Iberians have continued to immigrate to the United States. Despite its economic growth, Spain's gradual industrialization has driven away many who prefer the rural life. During the last three decades, the Portuguese have been among the largest immigrant groups in the United States. An estimated 161,000 arrived between 1959 and 1977.

Most Iberian emigrants have settled in Latin America or the United States. However, thousands of Portuguese moved to Canada in the 1950s and 1960s when the Canadian government signed an agreement with Portugal to import workers for farms and railroad construction sites in Quebec. An industrial boom after World War II had attracted Canadian workers away from physical labor into better-paying jobs in the city. However, the Portuguese soon moved to the cities, too. By 1961, there were 12,000 Portuguese in Toronto, 4,000 in Vancouver, and 3,000 in Montreal, most working in factories in the service trades. By the spring of 1976, a total of 220,000 Portuguese were living in Canada. Of those, 62 percent had come from the Azores, the remainder from the mainland.

But whether they came in 1910 or 1986, arrived by boat or by plane, all of the immigrants entered a world very different from the one they had left behind.

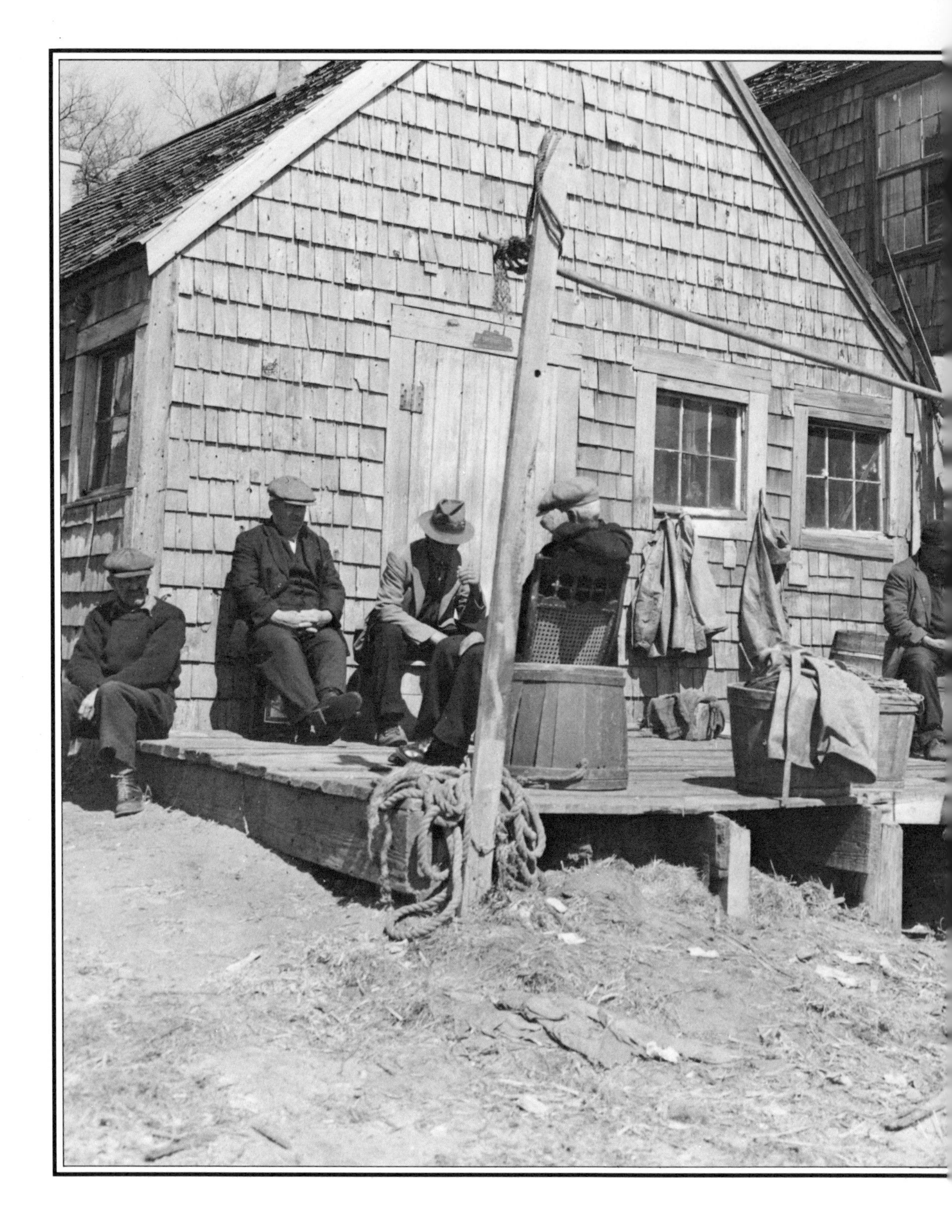

In the spring of 1942, Portuguese-American fishermen in Provincetown, Massachusetts, chat and bask in the sun in front of the shack where they store their equipment.

NEW LIVES IN AMERICA

Once they left the ships that brought them to America, the Iberians headed for settlements where they could join their countrymen who had arrived earlier. With the help of family and friends, they found jobs and homes, but they learned quickly that the streets were not paved with gold and that they would have to start at the bottom of the economic and social ladder. Clinging together in the midst of strangers who spoke a different language and had different customs, they worked hard to establish their place among them.

In New England

The greatest number of Iberians settled on the East Coast, where they found jobs in factories and on small farms. By 1920, there were 106,000 Portuguese in the United States, two-thirds of them living in Massachusetts, Rhode Island, and Connecticut. Nearly all were from the Azores, particularly the islands of Faial, Pico, São Jorge, and Flores. So many settled in New Bedford, Massachusetts, that it was nicknamed the Portuguese Capital of the United States.

Many of the Portuguese immigrants took up jobs fishing or working in related industries in Provincetown or Gloucester, Massachusetts. Some of the Portuguese in New England went to work as hired hands on local farms, saving their money so that they could rent a share for themselves and eventually buy their own land. Americans were impressed with the farming skills of the Portuguese. Accustomed to coaxing crops from the overworked land of their home islands, the Azoreans applied the same techniques to New England's rocky soil, raising potatoes in Portsmouth and berries in Cape Cod and transforming Martha's Vineyard from a sand-hill into a blossoming garden.

But between 1870 and 1920 the majority of Portuguese immigrants found work in the textile mills of New Bedford, Fall River, Lowell, and Lawrence, in Massachusetts; Providence, Rhode Island; and other southern New England towns. As Jerry Williams wrote in *And Yet They Come*, mill work was suited for the uneducated and unskilled Portuguese: "To be a bobbin boy, doffer, carder, comber, sweeper, spooler or any one of the other numerous semi-skilled occupations involved in manufacturing material from fiber did not require understanding the principles of hydraulic power or the operation of a mechanical loom; all that was necessary was to be able to stay awake and perform a tedious repetitious task in an unpleasant environment for ten or twelve hours a day."

Many of the people who toiled in the mills continued to dream of one day owning a farm of their own, but only a few were able to make that dream come true. By the late 1930s, the mills were beginning to shut down as it became cheaper to produce textiles elsewhere, and the workers had to find other jobs. Some gained employment in stores or as city employees. Others moved to areas where new factories were opening up; still others went home to Portugal. There were few rags-to-riches stories among the Portuguese in New England. It usually took a generation or two for families to rise even to the ranks of the lower middle class.

California Farmers

Although the largest concentration of Portuguese was on the East Coast, thousands headed west to California, where most worked on ranches and dairy farms. Others became involved in Southern California's commercial fishing industry. In the Monterey region, they joined the growing fish-canning businesses. The second largest group of Portuguese in the United States settled in the area around Oakland, California. In 1911, the *Saturday Evening Post* reported that "San Leandro, a little outside of Oakland, is a city of orchards and gardens and is almost as Portuguese as Lisbon itself." Home to 4,000 Portuguese inhabitants in 1892, San Leandro boasted 12,260 Portuguese residents by 1920. Most came from the western Azores, but there were also some Madeirans and Cape Verdians. Few were from the mainland. The Portuguese gradually spread out from the Oakland area into the Santa Clara Valley, the San Joaquin Valley, and Sacramento.

The majority of Portuguese farmers went into the dairy business. By 1939, Portuguese dairymen controlled 75 percent of the cattle business in California—nearly 450,000 head, worth more than $30 million. Milk production was valued at $24 million.

Owners of large dairy farms sometimes divided their property into smaller farms, which were operated by tenant farmers on a share basis. The owner provided the land, buildings, and cows, and the tenant provided the

Portuguese dairy farmers in California in 1910. The Portuguese ultimately came to dominate California's dairy industry.

labor, dairy utensils, horses, wagons, and furniture for his house. Typically, the successful Portuguese dairy farmer in California had worked as a milker on a tenant farm operated by other Portuguese, often relatives or acquaintances from home, until he had enough money to become a tenant farmer himself. Then he worked to save up enough capital to buy his own herd and a dairy farm. In addition to raising cows, the farmer produced most of his family's food on his land, growing vegetables and fruits and raising pigs for meat.

Imported Labor

The sugar industry had become important in Hawaii after the American Civil War. The growers initially relied on Chinese labor, but eventually the Chinese began to move elsewhere in search of less strenuous and more lucrative employment. Beginning in 1878, the Hawaiian government arranged to import large numbers of Portuguese as contract laborers. They generally brought the workers' families over as well in order to encourage their hired hands to stay.

Within 10 years, 12,000 Madeirans and São Miguelans from the Azores had come to Hawaii. Although most had no experience in the cane fields, they adapted to plantation life. After the fall of the Portuguese monarchy in 1910, another 2,000 came from continental Portugal, but they soon moved on to California. As their plantation contracts expired, many of the laborers went into other lines of work, either in the cities of Hawaii or in California. Some also took advantage of a homestead act that allowed them to buy public lands around Honolulu at low prices. Spanish workers were also brought to Hawaii to work in the cane fields. About 8,000 of them journeyed to the islands between 1906 and 1913. In order to avoid the government authorities of Spain, most were smuggled out by way of Gibraltar and were transported to Hawaii in overloaded ships. Nearly all left the plantations as soon as they were able. Most settled near San Francisco, California.

(continued on page 65)

FAMILY AND FAITH

(Overleaf) Portuguese-American children march in a parade in New Bedford, Massachusetts, on the Feast of the Blessed Sacrament. Family and faith are the critical elements that unite the Iberian-American community.

Attired in the colorful dress of the homeland (above), Portuguese Americans celebrate their past and culture, including their heritage as farmers (left), at the annual Portuguese Festival in Little Compton, Rhode Island. At the annual festival in Santa Fe, Spanish Americans celebrate the memory of Don Diego de Vargas, a colonial governor who won a decisive victory over New Mexico's Indians in 1692 (below).

The Portuguese maintain an enduring relationship with the sea. Portuguese Americans in Sandy Hook, New Jersey, enjoy spending a day with family and friends at the shore (above and bottom right), where they fish, eat and drink, and socialize. Some of the oldest and most culturally cohesive Spanish-American communities in the United States are in New Mexico; many of their residents are farmers, as their descendants have been for generations (top right).

Religious holidays are often the occasions for parades and celebration in the Iberian-American community. (At right) Portuguese Americans carry a statue of the Blessed Virgin during the Feast of Saint Senhor da Pedra in New Bedford; religious statues also play a central role in the annual Blessing of the Fleet in New Stonington, Connecticut (below), and Provincetown, Massachusetts (far right).

Portuguese-American youths reenact the holy family's search for shelter in a religious procession in New Bedford, Massachusetts. Such rituals are crucial in helping the Iberian-American community maintain its sense of ethnic identity.

A Portuguese woman carries a basketful of freshly baked bread on the Hawaiian island of Kauai, circa 1900.

(continued from page 56)

Iberians also worked in the sugarcane fields of Louisiana. They came in groups, with several hundred arriving in the 1840s and 230 more, including children, landing at New Orleans in 1872 with 3-year contracts to work on the plantations along the Latourche River. Working conditions were so bad, however, that most of the workers ran away within months to New Orleans or Cuba. The 1860 census showed 109 Portuguese living in New Orleans, which made it one of the few places in the South with a measurable Portuguese population.

Basque Sheepherders

Although a substantial number of Basques followed the example of the Iberians who remained in New York, their first stop in the New World, most followed a different path, playing a unique role among the immigrants of the late 19th and early 20th century as the sheepherders of the American West. Generally, the French Basques went to California, Arizona, central Nevada, New Mexico, Colorado, Wyoming, and Montana; the Spanish Basques, mostly from the region of Vizcaya, went to northern Nevada, Oregon, and Idaho. Although the two groups remained separate in most

Many members of the small Spanish-American community of Louisiana made their living as fur trappers. Shown here are Spanish-American trappers gathered at the general store on Delacroix Island for a fur auction in January 1941.

instances, they developed a similar way of life. Since the Basques tended to be solitary, independent workers, herding was a logical choice of occupation. It also offered the advantage of not requiring any knowledge of English, but it was a lonely way to live. Typically, the herder was responsible for a thousand or more sheep, moving them from low-elevation winter grazing areas up into the hills in the summer and caring for them through the lambing and shearing season. The enterprising herder worked his way up to camp tender and, as he was often paid in sheep, acquired animals of his own in three or four years and went into business for himself. If successful, he could sell his herd in a few years and return home a wealthy man. But to reach that point, the Basque sheepherders had to overcome many difficulties—bad weather, angry cattlemen, diseases that could wipe out their sheep, coyotes and mountain lions, dry years when there was no feed, and the vicissitudes of the marketplace. Herders who trusted their employers to hold on to their monthly wages were sometimes left with nothing when the owners went broke or cheated them. The intense solitude of their existence often played havoc with a herder's sanity, and suicide among the herders was not uncommon.

The center of activity for the Basque herder was the Basque hotel. Eventually, every major area of Basque settlement had such a hotel, run by a Basque man who served as friend, father, translator, employment agent, lawyer, financier, and matchmaker. The hotels served as the Basques' homes when they were not on the range and as a place to store clothes and possessions. The herders often trusted the hotel owner with their money, and he served as an intermediary when they purchased land or had other dealings with the English-speaking community.

Contrary to belief, only a small number of Basques were sheepherders in Iberia. Some Basques immigrated to South America first and learned about open-range herding on the plains there. By the 1880s, the sheep industry in South America was in decline, so the Basques headed north. However, the majority of Basque immigrants did not become sheepherders until after they arrived in the United States. They succeeded because as self-sufficient farmers in Iberia they had learned how to care for livestock, they were used to hard work, and they were willing to undergo extreme hardship. In the American West, Basque sheepherders had little competition for jobs, and they quickly came to dominate the industry. By the second half of the 19th century, many

A Basque family in Oregon in the early 1900s. Many Basques settled in the West and Northwest, where they could obtain work as sheepherders and where the need to learn English was not as great.

A Basque shepherd patrols his herd.

Americans automatically assumed that any Basque in the United States worked as a sheepherder.

By the early days of the 20th century there was less open land available for sheep to graze on, and Basques began to find other work. The immigration quotas imposed in the 1920s severely decreased the number of Basques coming to the United States, and the Taylor Grazing Act of 1934 virtually eliminated open-range land. Many Basques returned home and spread the word that there was no work available in the United States. By the 1940s, there was such a shortage of sheepherders that ranchers in Nevada and Idaho petitioned the government for help. Several special measures were passed to allow Basque herders to come to the United States for three-year stints. In the 1950s, approximately 1,000 Basques journeyed to the United States to work as herders. After their three-year term was up, many wound up staying on as farmers.

Other Occupations

Most of the immigrants from Iberia were poorly educated peasants, but the Spaniards who immigrated to the United States in the early 20th century generally had more money and education than the typical immigrant of the day. Most came with skills in a craft or profession, and many had been in the United States before.

A significant number of Spanish immigrants settled in New York City. Although few of them spoke English, they had an advantage because of the large number of Spanish-speaking Latin Americans already living in the United States. Most were able to find jobs teaching Spanish or doing the same type of work they had done in Spain. Poorer and less educated Spaniards opened ethnic shops or joined the Portuguese and other immigrants in the cotton mills. Large numbers of Spaniards also headed west to raise cattle or farm. In the early 1900s, Florida joined New York City as a center of the Spanish-American community. Spaniards were attracted by its closeness to Cuba and the Cuban cigar industry. By 1930 the Spanish community in the city of Tampa had grown to 8,383 and constituted slightly more than 8 percent of the city's total population.

Coping with a New World

The Iberians who immigrated to North America between 1850 and 1950 found their new life difficult in many ways. They faced poverty, strange customs, and a new language, all of which served to constantly remind them that they were far from home. An Azorean man who moved to Massachusetts recalled that he could not get over how much colder the weather was there. Some Spanish and Portuguese immigrants in New England and elsewhere had to cope with freezing temperatures and snow for the first time in their life.

Food was another component of daily life that the Iberian immigrants found different. Accustomed to growing everything they ate, immigrants who lived in the cities were puzzled by the markets and the unfamiliar edibles they found there. Because many of their favorite foods and dietary staples were not available, they had to learn to eat differently. Azoreans, for example, had to replace goat's milk with cow's milk and corn bread with white bread.

Although Iberian immigrants often lived at first in neighborhoods with fellow Iberians, compatriots often spoke different dialects, making it difficult for them to understand each other. The Iberians tried to settle with fellow immigrants from the same island or province. Among the Portuguese, islanders tended to shy away from mainlanders. Groups from different areas fought over differences in language and would not let their young men and women court each other.

In the New World, even the church, which had been such an important force in the Iberian villages, seemed foreign to them, with services conducted in English and many rituals from the old country abandoned or changed. Many immigrant communities paid for the transportation of priests who would say mass in Portuguese or Basque or Spanish and keep the old customs alive.

Discrimination

Because of their lack of education and the quite understandable confusion they exhibited in adjusting to their new life, Iberian immigrants were often seen by other Americans as ignorant, simpleminded, and superstitious. When their children went to school, they were labeled as backward because of their inability to immediately understand lessons taught in English.

Other prejudice focused on alleged racial differences. Many American whites looked down on the dark-skinned Cape Verdians, and some even believed that all Portuguese were "colored" and hence inferior. Such discrimination permeated and divided the immigrant community. Alarmed by the prejudice leveled against the Cape Verdians, many Portuguese tried to conceal their heritage for fear they would be lumped together with their countrymen. In Providence, where the majority of Cape Verdians lived in tenements on the city's east side, a 1920 survey showed that the "white Portuguese" (mainlanders) sought to live apart from their "black" compatriots.

Basque sheepherders also experienced discrimination. At a time when the competition for grazing land was fierce in the West, the Basques were not well liked by American cattlemen whose lands they crossed while moving their sheep from one grazing area to the next. The herders were seen by the general population as strange and foreign because of their long, solitary stints with their herds and because of their tendency to socialize primarily with other Basques. Often referred to as "dirty black bascos," they were also called "tramp sheepmen" because they had no definite home but wandered where the weather and the grass were good for their sheep. Because they planned to eventually return home with the money they had saved, most herders did not become citizens or buy land, further increasing their isolation.

Tenement Life

While the Basques were struggling to make their way on the open range, urban Iberian Americans grappled with their own problems. In *The Portuguese Americans*, Leo Pap describes a typical family's situation in Lowell, Massachusetts, in the early 1900s: The father earned $10 for 56 hours' work each week. Rent in a squalid tenement was $6 a month; food for the family cost $7.60 a week, leaving less than $4 each month for any other expenses.

The predicament described above was not atypical. Factory workers' wages were low, and their living and working conditions were often unappealing, unsafe, and unsanitary. Immigrant groups that had been established in the United States longer than the Iberians looked down on the newer arrivals. In the mills, the Iberians held the lowest positions and earned less money than the French Canadians, Poles, Irish, and Italians who had settled in New England before them. Typically, every able-bodied member of an Iberian family was forced to seek employment in the mills in order to pay for rent and food. Women who had never held jobs outside the home before went to work each day, and children were held out of school to work in the mills. The families lived in two- and three-story tenement houses crowded with other immigrants, often from the same island or village.

The crowded living conditions and long hours of factory work took their toll. The Portuguese communities in New Bedford and Fall River in 1910 had the highest infant-mortality rates in the nation—20 percent, double the national average. Portuguese immigrant communities also suffered from a higher incidence of tuberculosis, cholera, smallpox, and other deadly diseases.

Although the living conditions of those working in the urban factories were bad, it is still likely that the

Basque shepherds pack up their gear and prepare to break camp at the close of lambing season. The trailers are drawn by horses.

In the spring of 1942, several months after the United States entered World War II, a pensive Portuguese-American woman contemplates photos of her sons, all of whom were serving in the U.S. armed forces at the time.

immigrants' situation was better than it had been in Europe, for the possibility of change existed, if not for the immigrant generation, then for their children. As the labor movement grew in strength, wages rose and working conditions improved. Educated in American schools, the children of the immigrants learned English, the most important step toward greater opportunity. After World War II, immigrants who had served in the military qualified for real estate loans and were able to buy homes for themselves.

Iberians working on farms in California often had an easier time adjusting, in part because their life did not differ as greatly from what they had known at home. California's climate was much more similar to the homeland's than was New England's, and farming was work to which they were long accustomed. The relative isolation of farming communities, however, in some ways slowed the process of assimilation, as Iberians living there had less immediate need to learn English and merge with the mainstream community.

USA

A Portuguese Girl Scout troop in New Bedford in 1942.

BECOMING AMERICANS

The immigrant who has just arrived in a new country is likely to find everything around him frightening and confusing, and he can hardly be blamed for seeking out those who speak the same language and practice familiar customs. Over time, things become less foreign, less intimidating, and the immigrant begins to explore the new world around him. Sometimes this process can take several generations.

Initially, most Iberian immigrants were no different. They lived in the same neighborhoods and went to work in the same factories as their countrymen, or they found jobs on farms or ranches owned by their fellow Portuguese, Spanish, or Basques. Once established in America, they sent for their relatives and friends. Many immigrants never learned English. As long as they dealt primarily with their compatriots, there was little need. They spoke their native tongue at home and at work, and they married fellow immigrants from the same country—often from the same village. Most male Basque immigrants, for example, married Basque women. William Douglass and João Bilbao wrote in their book *Amerikanuak* that in 70 out of 73 Basque marriages recorded at the Winnemucca, Nevada, courthouse between 1895 and 1915, both partners were Basques. But things usually changed in the second generation. Once the children of immigrants went to school, they brought the English language and American culture home with them. The children and especially the grandchildren of immigrants also made friends with other nationalities. Many married people from outside their ethnic group, people who did not share the same customs and history. In spite of their parents' efforts to retain the old ways, the children and especially the grandchildren of immigrants often felt more American than Iberian.

Faced with pressure and discrimination both subtle and overt from their American peers, the children of immigrants were often anxious to shed the ways of the old country. To become more "American," many anglicized their names or adopted variations they had been given by immigration officials who could not pronounce their Iberian names. For example, Pereira became Perry, and Correa became Curry. Some also translated their names to their English counterparts. Alves was changed to White, Madeira to Wood, Pavao to Peacock. The children of immigrants became bilingual, using English outside the home and speaking their native language to parents and relatives. The third generation often learned only a few scattered words of their grandparents' tongue, and by the fourth generation the language of the homeland was largely forgotten.

Families Change

Immigrating and assimilating changed the family unit. In the homeland, Iberians often lived in extended family groups, with grandparents, cousins, and other relatives living under the same roof with parents and children. An important part of most Catholic families was the godparents—relatives or friends chosen when a baby was baptized to serve as spiritual parents, watching over the child's religious education and providing comfort and assistance whenever needed.

The typical American family unit, by contrast, consisted only of parents and their children. By Iberian standards, American children, particularly females, enjoyed far more independence than was granted youngsters in the old country. The expectation of immigrant parents that their children would behave according to Old World standards led to conflict. This gap between generations only widened with the second and third generations' increased familiarity with American culture, which often remained essentially "foreign" to parents and grandparents.

In America, the roles played by Iberian women changed dramatically. In Iberia, women never worked outside the home, but in America many were forced to seek employment. With their new status as wage earners, women often gained increased authority in the household. In *The Portuguese Americans*, Leo Pap maintained that emancipation for women came with emigration. A 1905 survey conducted in Massachusetts showed that 43 percent of all foreign-born women over the age of 16 worked in the mills. Women worked on the farms of Rhode Island and the plantations of Hawaii as well. Still, the old ways did not change completely, and a man was usually regarded as the head of the family. To a certain extent, the women's lot remained the same, even for females of the second generation. Gerald A. Estep wrote in 1941: "In many Portuguese homes, the daughter is still merely an apprentice to the mother in the ways of being an obedient, faithful, diligent wife. When her required school days are over, she is expected to remain in the home until she is courted and married." At about the same time Estep was writing, however, a Portuguese woman was elected mayor of San Leandro.

Church and State

Although many immigrants changed their names, learned a new language, found new freedom within the family unit, and took jobs that were different from

This photograph of Our Lady of Good Voyage Catholic Church in Gloucester, Massachusetts, was taken in 1943. At the time, the church's congregation was primarily made up of Portuguese fishermen and their families. The statue of the Madonna atop the church holds a fishing schooner in its left hand.

anything they had done before, they looked to the church as the one constant in their new life. In some ways, the Catholic church in America was identical to that of Portugal and Spain, but there were subtle differences. In the villages of Iberia, the church reflected social relationships and myriad cultural traditions. The priest was often the most powerful person in the village. Iberian immigrants soon learned that the church in America rarely was given as high a priority. In Portugal, for example, the government built and maintained churches, but in North America the parishioners were expected to support them. Although Roman Catholic services were said in Latin around the world until the 1960s, language was also sometimes a barrier, for in the United States, sermons and announcements were usually read in English.

But the church did add a familiar element to the lives of Iberian immigrants. Iberian-American communities raised money to build their own churches and, within the limits imposed by the church hierarchy, sought to recruit priests who spoke their language. The churches in such parishes were often decorated with statues of saints who were particularly revered by Iberians and with patriotic symbols. The churches served as centers for celebrations and rituals similar to those the immigrants had known at home.

Like the Portuguese and the Spanish, the Basques were uneasy about joining "American" Catholic congregations and preferred clergy who knew their language and their ways. Sometimes traveling priests rode miles to hold services for Basque congregations. The Basque sheepherders, who had attended mass regularly in their homeland, found that their geographical isolation made it impossible to do so in America except for major feast days, weddings, and funerals, and they prayed alone on the range in between. Funerals were particularly important to the Basques, who conducted a long series of rituals, banquets, and sacrificial offerings

A nun gives a geography lesson to her young Portuguese-American charges at a Roman Catholic school in New Bedford in 1943.

when someone died. In America, however, a dead person was given a much more hasty burial unless a Basque priest could be found to pray and sing for his or her soul.

Iberians as Citizens

Although they sought to participate in religious activities, the Iberians were slow to involve themselves in other community endeavors, particularly politics. Because most Basque immigrants planned to eventually return to their homeland, they did not become citizens, often living in the United States for decades before deciding to apply for naturalization. To this day, Basque participation in American politics has been slight.

The same was true of the Portuguese and the Spanish. In the 1930s only the Mexicans became citizens at a lower rate. Most Portuguese arrived with a deep distrust of government and were unaccustomed to voting or otherwise participating in the political process. Illiteracy prevented many from trying to qualify for citizenship. However, the growth of the labor movement in the 1930s exposed many immigrants to political activity, and over time many employers required that immigrants be citizens before they could be hired. American citizenship also came to be seen as a form of protection for those

Hawaii was one area of Portuguese settlement in America where early immigrants took an active part in government. Two members of the 1917 territorial senate there were Portuguese: Manuel Pacheco (top row, far left) and Sylvester Correa (middle row, second from left). By 1925, eight members of the territorial legislature were Portuguese Americans.

who had left their homeland illegally. The U.S. government sponsored several successful citizenship drives, and other Iberians became citizens at the urging of their children.

Self-help Societies

Isolated as they often were within the larger American community, Spanish and Portuguese immigrants were forced to rely on each other for help in times of crisis. The characteristic form that this need for mutual aid engendered was the so-called benevolent society. Such societies at first admitted only males, and their initial purpose was to raise money to help members and their families in times of sickness or death. In many cities, their activities grew to include orientation programs for new immigrants, educational programs, and ethnic festivals. Some even sponsored marching bands and athletic teams. Occasionally, they raised money to be sent to the homeland in times of famine, earthquake, and other natural disasters. The first Iberian benevolent society was founded in 1868. Thirty years later, there were 800 such societies with 100,000 members in 21 states.

Among the largest of the benevolent societies are the Portuguese Continental Union of California (UPEC), which was established in 1880 and now has 77 branches, and the Portuguese Continental Union of the United States of America, founded in Plymouth, Massachusetts, in 1925. Eventually, Iberian women formed their own societies.

The societies encouraged their members to become involved in the larger community. The Portuguese-American League, founded in 1911 in Oakland, California, urged immigrants to acquire citizenship and participate in local politics. That same year, the first Portuguese American was elected to the California State Assembly.

The oldest Spanish benevolent organization is the Centro Español (Spanish Center) of New York. It offers cultural activities, legal services, and employment list-

BOLETIM DA U.P.E.C.

UNIÃO PORTUGUEZA DO ESTADO DA CALIFORNIA

EL-REI
E'CONVIDADO
A
ACCEITAR
A
PRESIDENCIA SUPREMA
HONORARIA

COPIA
DO CONVITE
QUE FOI
ENVIADO
A
S. M. FIDELISSIMA
EL-REI

The front page of the Bulletin *of the Portuguese Continental Union of California for October 1, 1902, consists of an invitation to King Don Carlos of Portugal (pictured) to serve as the association's first honorary president.*

ings and serves as a social center and mutual-aid society. There are more than a dozen such organizations in and around New York City.

Spread out over a larger geographical area, the Basques formed benevolent societies later than the other Iberian groups. Often, their hotels served as cultural centers. But by 1920 there were 10,000 Basques living in New York City, where they formed clubs for mutual aid and social activities. Established in 1941, the Centro Vasco remains a Basque social center, offering ethnic dinners and card games and sponsoring a folk dance group. French and Spanish Basques have usually formed separate groups with separate activities, although there is some crossover.

Like other immigrant groups, Iberian Americans published their own newspapers. By the 1880s, Portuguese-language newspapers existed in California, Hawaii, and New England. Typically, these carried local news as well as items of interest in the homeland. Even within the immigrant community their readership was small, mainly because so many Portuguese were illiterate. The only Portuguese daily newspaper of long standing, *Diário de Notícias*, was published in New Bedford by João R. Rocha between 1919 and 1973. As of 1980, there were five major Portuguese-American weekly newspapers, aimed at the Portuguese communities of San Francisco, California; Newark, New Jersey; Bristol, Rhode Island; and New Bedford and Fall River, Massachusetts.

The first Portuguese radio program in the United States aired in 1922 in New Bedford, but most Portuguese radio has originated in California. Artur V. Avila, a newspaperman from the Azorean island of Pico, created the first daily Portuguese radio program in Oakland, California, in 1931. By 1958, there were 17 Portuguese radio programs in the state. "Castelos Romanticos," which Avila produced with his wife, Celeste, was one of the most popular. The Portuguese community deeply mourned Avila's passing in 1962.

Because of the large number of Spanish speakers from Central and South America who have immigrated to the United States, Spanish Americans have enjoyed ready access to Spanish newspapers, radio programs, and televison shows. Their focus may not be on Spain, but Spanish speakers need not feel isolated from news and information about the larger Spanish community. Particularly in New York City, Florida, the Southwest, and California, Spanish-language publications are readily available. The Basques have had fewer channels of communication available to them in their native language. Even in the homeland, the language does not have a strong literary tradition, and relatively few books, except for religious texts, have been written in Basque. Several Basque immigrants attempted to start newspapers in the late 1800s, but none lasted more than a few years. A monthly publication entitled *Voice of the Basques* was begun in Boise, Idaho, in 1974, but it is written mostly in English. Weekly radio broadcasts in Basque in Elko and Winnemucca, Nevada; Boise, Idaho; and Buffalo, Wyoming, have proved more successful.

A tree carving of a man on horseback done by a Basque in Nevada. Such carvings are a popular form of Basque folk art.

Maintaining Ethnic Pride

Iberian Americans have adopted many American ways, but they have also retained much from their homeland. Most of their numerous festivals and annual celebrations, for example, center around traditional religious holidays or commemorate important events in the history of Iberia.

The term *festa* is used for nearly any kind of Portuguese party or picnic in the United States. Most festas honor the patron saint of a town, village, or parish or commemorate religious miracles. After the religious ceremony comes dancing, feasting, and courting among the young.

One of the most popular and colorful Portuguese festivals is the Holy Ghost Festival (Festa do Espirito Santo), celebrated at Pentecost. Although stories of the

Within the Iberian-American community, time-honored traditions survive amid the sometimes jarring realities of modern American life. Here, a parade in celebration of one of the festas *of the Azorean community of San Leandro, California, moves past businesses and telephone and electric wires along one of the town's avenues.*

festa's origin vary considerably, most concern the pious Isabel of Aragon, wife of Dom Diniz, a 14th-century Portuguese monarch. According to legend, Isabel's heartfelt prayers saved her people from starvation. In gratitude for God's miraculous intervention, Isabel relinquished her crown to a peasant girl, as she had promised the Lord she would do. Most Holy Ghost festivals include a procession, the crowning of a queen, a church service, and a day or weekend of eating, singing, and dancing. Auctions are held, with profits going to the poor.

The Santo Cristo Festival, held in Fall River, is celebrated by Azoreans from São Miguel. Activities revolve around the worship of a statue depicting Jesus Christ exposed to the jeering crowds when he was taken before Pontius Pilate. A number of miracles have been claimed in connection with the statue, and there are replicas in many Portuguese churches in the United States. People come from all over the country to Fall River for the celebration, which is held the fifth Sunday after Easter.

Festas are also held each summer in honor of Our Lady of Fatima, a miraculous vision of the Virgin Mary that appeared to three shepherd children in Fatima,

Portugal. Other popular festas include Nossa Senhora dos Milagres (Our Lady of Miracles), a September celebration of the patroness of the Cape Verdian island of Corvo; Festa do Santissimo Sacramento (Feast of the Most Holy Sacrament), a Madeiran festival held in New Bedford in August; and Our Lady of Good Voyage, which is held in Gloucester every June and includes the blessing of the fishing fleet by the archbishop of Boston.

In addition to religious holidays, Portuguese Americans commemorate December 1, 1640, the date Portugal achieved its independence from Spain, and October 5, 1910, the day when the Portuguese monarchy was replaced by a republican government. They also celebrate June 10, Portugal Day, as a time of reaffirmation of the ties between Portuguese in the United States and in Europe.

The Basques hold a number of annual celebrations. Picnics and contests of strength are popular. In Buffalo, Wyoming, groups of Basques gathered in the early 1900s to play handball on property owned by Jean Esponda. By 1918, the get-together had become an annual tradition, with a picnic and handball tournament held in the summer ranges of the nearby Bighorn Mountains. In 1929, the first annual Sheepherders' Ball was held in Boise, Idaho. The balls are still held each winter, with proceeds going to charity.

Because of the mistreatment the Basques received, their annual celebrations were often closed affairs to which outsiders were rarely invited. More recently, the Basques have opened their celebrations to the public. In June 1959, the first Western Basque Festival was held in Sparks, Nevada. More than 5,000 people attended the event, which included a banquet of Basque food, folk dancing, music, sheepdog competitions, and athletic contests. Tug-of-war, wood chopping, and stone lifting are extremely popular among Basque men, who value physical strength. The festival has become the largest single gathering of Basques in the American West, and it has been imitated at other locations. Since 1964, Elko,

Nevada, has been the site for the National Basque Festival, held every July 4.

Iberian Culture in America

As did other immigrants, the Iberians brought their traditional music, dances, sports, and foods to America. Music is a major part of any Iberian social event. The Portuguese are fond of *cantoria ao desafio,* in which two people alternately sing improvised verses while accompanying themselves on a *vida,* or Portuguese-style guitar. The one who sings the longest in good rhythm without faltering while sticking to the designated subject is declared the winner. Storytelling songs that have been passed down from generation to generation are another integral part of the Portuguese musical tradition, although they have proved less popular with the younger generation. The Portuguese brought with them several instruments, including the six-string vida, the five-string *rajáo,* and a small, four-string guitar called a *braguinha* or *machete* in Madeira and known in America as the ukulele.

Dancing is also common at Iberian social events. Descendants of Portuguese immigrants fondly remember the *chamarrita,* a dance that is still a favorite among the older generation, especially those from Pico, Faial, and Flores. The dance is accompanied by a song of the same name. It begins with couples dancing separately in a kind of waltz or *mazurka;* then the men and women line up, joining hands and waltzing in the round: Couples waltz off separately; then each woman circles halfway around her partner. Finally, the men and women join one hand and hop around on the spot. The dance continues with variations, accentuated by intermittent chanting.

Other Portuguese dances include the *pezinho,* a round dance, and the *furado,* in which a line of women slip through a parallel line of men. Madeirans dance the syncopated *charamba, camacheiras,* and *mourisca;* continentals dance the *viva,* with women in the inner circle, men in the outer; and Cape Verdians enjoy the tangolike *morna*. Basques and Spaniards enjoy the *jota*, a line dance that can be done by individuals or couples. Clothed in white or black, with red sashes and berets, the dancers make a colorful picture at the annual celebrations.

Pelota, or *jai alai*, is the most popular sport in the Basque country. "There is not a village in the Basque country where some form of handball is not played, and with a passion," William Douglass and João Bilbao wrote in *Amerikanuak*, adding, "Pelota is to Basque youngsters what sandlot baseball is to their American counterparts." Somewhat similar to handball, jai alai is played on a three-walled court, called a *fronton*, with a hard rubber ball, the pelota, that is caught and hurled with a wicker basket, the *cesta*, attached to a player's arm. It is played by either 2 or 4 competitors at a time, and among skilled players the pelota sometimes achieves speeds of more than 130 miles per hour. In the United States, Basque players have been recruited to play in professional leagues in Miami, Florida; Bridgeport and Hartford, Connecticut; and Newport, Rhode Island.

Along with music and games, food and drink are an essential part of any Iberian celebration. Food is the highlight of any Basque party, which usually features lots

The Basque game of jai alai, *or* pelota, *requires a combination of catlike grace, extraordinary reflexes, tireless endurance, and raw power.*

of steak, barbecued lamb, spicy Basque beans, red wine, and coffee with brandy.

Many Basque hotels have been converted to restaurants in recent years. They serve *picon* punch, a traditional Basque drink, along with chicken, steak, lamb, pork, and shellfish. There are also tureens of homemade soup, platters of spaghetti with meat sauce, mountains of fried potatoes, and bottles of red wine, all served at long family-style tables. Usually, side dishes such as paella (rice with shellfish), chicken and meat with rice, oxtails, lamb stew, or liver with onions are included.

Portuguese restaurants have grown in popularity in recent years with the increased interest in ethnic cuisine. Among the most popular entrées served in such establishments is *porco a alentejana*, which consists of cubed pork with clams in a savory sauce. Typical Portuguese fare also includes many different codfish dishes (the Portuguese boast that they have 365 different ways to prepare cod), kale soup, sweet bread, and *linguiça* and *chouriço* sausages. Spanish restaurants in the United States serve seafood entrées with nut sauces, pasta dishes, lamb, and quail, along with many different kinds of *tapas*—fish or meat appetizers commonly served in the bars of Spain.

All of the Iberian groups are hearty drinkers of wine. The Basques are known for their *bota* bags, made of animal hide, which they hold up over their head in order to squirt wine down their throat. Many Portuguese and Spanish make wine at home to drink with meals. Basque shepherd Beltrán Paris recalled in his book *Beltrán, Basque Sheepman of the American West* that he ordered a truckload of grapes every year and made wine for himself and his herders. Some years, he made as much as 600 gallons.

Celebrating Iberian Heritage

Until the 1960s, many immigrants and their children felt the need to hide their "foreignness" in order to be accepted by the American people. In recent years, it has become acceptable and even fashionable to celebrate one's ethnic background. With the increase in ethnic awareness has come a renewed interest in preserving and celebrating the Iberian cultural heritage.

The Basques formed relatively few social clubs, in part because of the solitary way of life of so many of them, but in 1972 the North American Basque Organizations, Inc., united Basque groups from all over the West. The organization's emphasis is on socializing and recreation, in the form of dances, dinners, picnics, concerts, jai alai tournaments, and folk-dance recitals, although the organization also awards scholarships and raises money for donations to the needy. To promote the study of the Basque people and culture, the University of Nevada at Reno established a Basque studies program in 1967. The university also sponsors the most extensive Basque library outside of Europe. Boise State University in Idaho offers Basque-language classes and has sponsored trips to the Basque country.

A variety of organizations exist to preserve the Spanish heritage, including the Spanish American Cultural Heritage group in San Jose, California; the Hispanic Society of America; and the Hispanic Institute in New York City. As its name indicates, the Society of Spanish and Portuguese Historical Studies at the State University of New York deals with the two larger Iberian groups. Many colleges and universities offer Spanish and Portuguese studies. Portuguese-American clubs include the American Portuguese Society and the Cape Verdean League, both in New York, and the Luso-American Education Foundation in Oakland, California. One of the oldest Portuguese-American social clubs is the Sociedade Portuguesa Rainha Santa Isabel (the Portuguese Society of Queen Saint Isabel), which was founded in California in 1898 for women of Portuguese descent. It had 13,000 members in 1980.

Dominique Laxalt (in suit and tie), an immigrant from the Basque country, and his family. His son Robert (second from left) is a well-known author, and son Paul (second from right) has served as governor of Nevada and as a U.S. senator from that state.

IBERIAN CONTRIBUTIONS TO AMERICAN LIFE

Most Iberian immigrants did not become rich or famous. They were simply hardworking people who loved their family, their God, and their new country, but they have left their mark on American life in many ways.

Evidence of the early Spanish explorers and settlers can be found throughout the United States, not only in place names and words that have crept into the language but also in the cowboy culture considered so American. The Spanish brought the first cows and established the first ranches. The American cowboy inherited his trade, horse, outfit, lingo, and methods from the Spanish. Much of western mining and water-rights law also has Spanish roots.

In other ways, the contribution of Iberians has been less obvious. Although there have been some Iberian Americans who have achieved great success in business—William Wood, son of an Azorean immigrant, went on to found the American Woolen Company, which owned 59 mills at its peak in 1929; Joseph Fernandes built his parents' small grocery store into a chain of 30 supermarkets—the overall Iberian-American influence on business and the economy has been, as Leo Pap described it, "essentially a collective and anonymous one of relatively unskilled labor."

The products of a culture where physical labor was often valued more highly than intellectual activity, the Basques generally have not entered the professions. The brothers Robert and Paul Laxalt have probably achieved the greatest degree of fame, the former as a writer and the latter as governor of Nevada and U.S. senator from that state. Still, a number of highly talented and ambitious Iberian Americans have achieved significant individual success, winning fame and in some cases fortune while making important contributions to American cultural life.

Literature

The critic Aubrey Bell wrote that, with the exception of Greece, no small nation has produced as great literature as Portugal. Between 1919 and 1967, John Roderigo Dos Passos, a third-generation Portuguese American, carried on that tradition in the language of his forebears' adopted homeland, adding a distinctive and innovative voice to the flowering of American literature that occurred between the two world wars.

Born in Chicago, Illinois, in 1896, Dos Passos was the grandson of Manoel Dos Passos, an immigrant from the island of Madeira. John Roderigo was born out of wedlock. His father, John, Sr., was a wealthy and well-connected lawyer; his mother, Lucy Madison, proudly traced her ancestry back through several generations of Yankee stock. (His parents later married.) A bright and inquisitive child, John Roderigo excelled scholastically at preparatory school and at Harvard University, where he received honors for his literary ability. Following his graduation in 1916, Dos Passos volunteered to serve in the ambulance corps during World War I.

His experiences on the Continent during the "war to end all wars" inspired his first two novels, *One Man's Initiation* (1919) and *Three Soldiers* (1921), which won him fame and some degree of notoriety for his unflinching portrayal of the disillusionment felt by the men in the trenches. An extremely ambitious writer, Dos Passos insisted that literature concern itself with the pressing social and political issues of the day, and in his most important works, *Manhattan Transfer* (1925) and the three novels that together make up the *U.S.A.* trilogy (1930–36), he attempted to capture the essence, energy, and failings of modern American society while at the same time examining the historical forces that had created it. To do so, Dos Passos made use of techniques often associated with more introspective writers, such as stream of consciousness, as well as his own innovations, such as interspersing contemporary headlines, song lyrics, and the biographies of actual personages—Henry Ford, William Jennings Bryan, and others—throughout his fictional narrative. Politics interested Dos Passos almost as much as literature. Like many intellectuals of the time, in the 1920s he opposed the execution of Nicola Sacco and Bartolomeo Vanzetti, Italian immigrants and alleged anarchists who were convicted of committing murder while carrying out a robbery. Dos Passos believed that the two had been given an unfair trial and convicted more on the basis of their politics than on evidence. In the 1930s, he actively supported the Loyalists during the Spanish civil war and helped raise money for medical supplies and humanitarian aid for the Spanish. Over time, as his literary reputation waned—he never repeated the success of *U.S.A.*—Dos Passos's politics grew increasingly conservative, and he found himself alienated from many of his former friends in the literary community. He died in 1970. Although seldom accorded the same stature as his contemporaries,

Portuguese-American writer John Dos Passos at work in the study of his home in Westmoreland, Virginia, in 1964.

Ernest Hemingway (who was, at different times, both a close friend and a bitter enemy) and William Faulkner, Dos Passos is still regarded as one of the important American writers of the 20th century.

Like Dos Passos, Truman Capote won his greatest fame for pioneering literary techniques. Of Spanish descent, Capote was born in New Orleans, Louisiana, in 1924. An extremely precocious child, possessed of enormous intelligence and given to fantasizing and storytelling, Capote had a chaotic childhood, due in part to his mother's instability, and did not receive extensive formal education. He decided on a literary career at a young age, and while only 24 published *Other Voices, Other Rooms*, a novel whose maturity of style stunned critics. Capote's fame grew throughout the 1950s and 1960s with the publication of another novel, *The Grass Harp*, a collection of short stories, *Tree of Night*, and especially the popular novella *Breakfast at Tiffany's*, but it did not reach its zenith until the 1966 publication of *In Cold Blood*, a recounting of the savage murder of a Kansas farm family by two drifters.

Capote called *In Cold Blood* a "non-fiction novel," by which he meant that he used the traditional narrative methods of the novel to tell the story of an actual event. The characters in the book were real people, called by their real names; all the events retold actually occurred. Capote's unflinching eye for detail and his precise but poetic prose succeeded in imparting the enormous tragedy of the crime as well as in making the murderers human, if not sympathetic. The product of years of exhaustive research, *In Cold Blood* helped give rise to the so-called New Journalism of the late 1960s and 1970s, but unlike such later practitioners as Tom Wolfe, Norman Mailer, and Hunter Thompson, Capote did not include himself as a character in his story. *In Cold Blood* won critical and popular acclaim, and its flamboyant author was lionized. An enthralling raconteur, Capote was the darling of New York high society until the publication, in *Esquire* magazine, of an unsparing satire of some of its

Flamboyant author Truman Capote in his early thirties, about 10 years before the success of In Cold Blood.

more famous members. He claimed that the piece was part of his masterwork, *Answered Prayers*, which he envisioned as a microscopic examination of the world of the rich and famous comparable to the work of the great French novelist Marcel Proust, but it made him a pariah among the haut monde, whose society he coveted. Afterward, the elfin Capote was notable more for his outrageous public persona, outspoken homosexuality, and debilitating bouts with alcohol and drug addiction than for his literary output. At his death in 1984, *Answered Prayers* remained unfinished.

The poet Juan Ramón Jiménez was of that generation of Spanish intellectuals who emigrated in order to escape the turmoil created by the Spanish civil war and the repression of the Franco regime that took power afterward. After sojourns in several other nations, including Cuba, the 66-year-old Jiménez accepted a professorship at the University of Maryland in 1947. Most of Jiménez's greatest works were written before he left Spain; most are elegiac and obsessive, concerned with the themes of spiritual love and death. Although his poetry earned him the Nobel Prize in literature in 1956, his most widely read work is a children's story first published in 1914, *Platero y yo* (Platero and I), an endearing tale about a donkey. Jiménez died in San Juan, Puerto Rico, in 1958.

King of the Marches

The marching band remains a symbol of American energy and endurance, and no individual contributed more to that peculiarly American musical configuration than John Philip Sousa. Known the world over for his marching songs, Sousa was born in Washington, D.C., in 1854. His Portuguese father, João Antonio de Sousa, played with the U.S. Marine Band for 25 years.

The March King, John Philip Sousa (on pedestal at center), posed with the U.S. Marine Band before a White House performance in 1890.

As a boy, John studied violin and trombone and began composing songs. When at age 13 he announced that he had decided to run away with the circus, his father enlisted him in the Marine Band instead. Sousa wound up directing the Marine Band from 1880 to 1892, when he resigned to start his own group. The Sousa band toured for 40 years, earning its founder worldwide fame for the marches he composed, including "Stars and Stripes Forever," "The Liberty Bell," "Semper Fidelis," "The Washington Post March," and "Hands Across the Sea." Before his death in 1932, Sousa also wrote operettas, piano suites, and instructional manuals for piano and drums and designed a curved tuba, the sousaphone, that is used in many marching bands.

On the Bench

Being named to the U.S. Supreme Court is a signal achievement for a jurist. It has also been, throughout history, a reason for pride on the part of the ethnic or gender group to which he or she belongs. The individual selected is often seen as a symbol of achievement for his people. To whatever extent Benjamin Nathan Cardozo, a Portuguese Jew, was seen by himself or others as a standard-bearer, there is little doubt that his was one of the foremost legal minds of his generation. Indeed, so widely acclaimed were his accomplishments that the appointment of the 62-year-old Cardozo to the Supreme Court in 1932 was devoid of the controversy that often accompanies such selections. And although his term on the high court lasted only six years, until his death in 1938, Cardozo is arguably one of the dozen most influential justices in history.

Cardozo seemed born to the bench. He entered the world in New York City in 1870, the son of an attorney and judge, and there is little indication that he ever considered devoting his life to anything but the law. He entered Columbia College (now University) at the age of

The well-reasoned opinions of Justice Benjamin Cardozo made him one of the most respected Supreme Court justices in the history of the United States.

15 and graduated with a master's degree in law 5 years later. Although he inspired intense personal devotion and loyalty, the soft-spoken and somewhat reticent Cardozo never married, and most of his energies were reserved for his work. Until 1913, he engaged in private practice, primarily in corporate and commercial work, and built an almost legendary reputation among his colleagues for his acumen. That year, he was persuaded to run for the New York Supreme Court. He won, and one month later he was appointed to the state's highest judicial body, the court of appeals.

Over the next 18 years, Cardozo's judicial opinions, characterized by unimpeachable knowledge of the law, a distinctive literary style, and clear reasoning that made the court's decision accessible even to the layman, won him an unprecedented reputation with the public. Fellow justices marveled at his ability to build a majority coalition from the often disparate opinions held by the other justices on the bench. When a U.S. Supreme Court seat became vacant in 1932, President Herbert Hoover did not, in the words of Justice Felix Frankfurter, "so much choose Cardozo as ratify the country's selection." Cardozo's 150 opinions written during his short stint on the Supreme Court remain influential because, again in Frankfurter's words, "he imparted distinction to whatever he touched, to cases great or small, to cases involving large public issues or turning on narrow technicality." After his death, Chief Justice Charles Evan Hughes delivered a fitting judicial epitaph: "No judge ever came to this Court more fully equipped by learning, acumen, dialectical skill, and disinterested purpose. He came to us in the full maturity of his extraordinary intellectual power, and no one on this bench has ever served with more untiring industry or more enlightened outlook."

Religion, Science, and Entertainment

Not surprisingly, many Iberian Americans have devoted their lives to the Catholic church. Particularly notable among these is Humberto S. Madeiros, who was born on the Azorean island of São Miguel. After moving with his family to Fall River in 1931, Madeiros swept floors at a textile mill for 62 cents a day, but he went on to earn a doctorate in theology at Catholic University in Washington, D.C., and was appointed pastor of a Fall River immigrant church in 1958. In 1970, he became the first non-Irish archbishop of Boston in 124 years. In 1973, Madeiros was made a cardinal of the Catholic church.

Among the Iberian-American scientists whose work has won them notice is Spanish American Luis W.

Alvarez, who won the 1968 Nobel Prize in physics for his work on the detection and behavior of subatomic particles. Previously, Alvarez had been lauded for developing a ground-controlled radar system for landing aircraft that was adopted for standard use by the U.S. Army Air Force in 1945 and for his work on the development of atomic weaponry. Severo Ochoa, who was born in Laureo, Spain, was awarded the 1959 Nobel Prize in medicine and physiology for his research concerning the laboratory synthesis of DNA and RNA, the basic genetic building blocks. Ochoa's experiments were conducted while he was working as a professor at the New York University College of Medicine in 1955.

Actors Martin Sheen (left) and his son Charlie at a rally against the Strategic Defense Initiative (also known as the Star Wars program) at the Riverside Research Institute in New York City in July 1987. In the 1980s, the elder Sheen has won almost as much fame for his political activism as for his acting.

Perhaps the Iberian Americans most recognizable to the majority of Americans are those who have achieved fame in the movies, on television, or in professional sports. The sultry silver-screen goddess of the 1930s and 1940s, Rita Hayworth, was born Margarita Carmen Cansino, the daughter of a Spanish vaudevillian and an English mother. The star of the film *Apocalypse Now* and numerous popular television movies, Martin Sheen, was born Ramón Estevez. He changed his name at a time when obvious ethnicity was viewed as a possible hindrance to a film career. One of his sons, Emilio, also an actor, has reclaimed the family name, although another son, Charlie Sheen, who starred in *Platoon* and *Wall Street*, has not. Actress Raquel Welch is the daughter of a Bolivian immigrant of Spanish descent and was born Raquel Tejada.

The most well known Iberian-American sports figure is the fiery five-time manager of the New York Yankees, Billy Martin, who was born Alfred Manuel Pesano in Berkeley, California, in 1928. After an 11-year playing career in which he distinguished himself more for hustle, grit, and on-the-field smarts than for outstanding ability, Martin went on to manage the Minnesota Twins, Detroit Tigers, Texas Rangers, Oakland Athletics, and New York Yankees. As a manager, Martin often achieved outstanding records with teams that were not expected to excel, and the heady, aggressive style of play that he perfected with the Oakland Athletics became known as Billyball. Although his arguments with umpires and fistfights with players and fans have often cast Martin in the role of antihero, there is little doubt that over the past 20 years he has been one of baseball's most adroit field generals.

A taut-veined Billy Martin pleads his case with umpire Drew Coble in April 1983, during Martin's third stint as manager of the New York Yankees. Martin's winning percentage as a manager ranks as one of the highest recorded over the last 30 years.

A young Portuguese-American girl at the annual Blessing of the Fleet in Provincetown, Massachusetts, in August 1976. The Iberians' Catholic faith has helped them preserve a strong sense of their ethnic identity in North America.

SUMMING UP

Most Iberian immigrants came to America with little more than a satchel of clothing and a dream of a better life. For many, those dreams have come true, if not for them, then for their children or their grandchildren, who have built on the foundations laid down by the first immigrants. Unlike their forebears, the descendants of the first immigrants feel free to pursue any career or way of life that appeals to them, unconstrained by poverty and lack of education. Iberian immigrants who had once viewed education with suspicion, considering it a frivolous escape from the hard work that needed to be done, came to recognize the value of school. Many Portuguese first began to appreciate education when the depression all but eliminated employment opportunities for adolescents, affording them the chance to stay in school. The Spanish also came to value education. In 1920, only 20 percent of Spanish Americans graduated from high school, but by 1970 the number had increased to 70 percent. Forty percent of Spanish-American men and 30 percent of Spanish-American women went on to college. Between 1950 and 1970, a growing proportion of Spanish Americans got better-paying and higher-status jobs as they became more educated and moved into the cities. By 1970, 1 in 10 Spanish Americans was a professional.

The Portuguese, who started at the bottom of the economic ladder, are still generally a low-income group, but their economic status has also improved. Descendants of the Portuguese immigrants generally occupy the lower middle class, with a good sprinkling in the middle and upper middle classes. Many Azorean farmers still maintain a rural way of life, but large numbers, especially in California, have sold their farms at a profit and moved into industrial occupations.

Although still identified with the sheep industry, the Basques have entered many different fields, including dairy work in Southern California, gardening in San Francisco, selling sourdough bread in central and southern California, and working as lumberjacks in Oregon. Many are still involved in some aspect of animal husbandry, and others are small businessmen. Because of their reputation for hard work, loyalty, and honesty, they are in demand as employees in mining companies, construction firms, and sawmills.

Immigrants Who Returned Home

A large percentage of the Iberians who came to the United States intended to return home eventually to buy land, get married, or retire. Yet, as Jerry Williams discussed in his study *And Yet They Come*, "as it turned out, many of these immigrants never achieved their wishes of returning home. As time went by, they became accustomed to the New World that destiny had forced upon them, and their bones were buried here and there, along with those sacrifices and deeds left unsung."

Although many gave up the hope of returning home, a substantial number did go back to visit or to stay. From 1921 to 1965, when immigration was limited by U.S. government quotas, returnees to Portugal and Spain outnumbered new arrivals in the United States. The voyages between the United States and the Iberian countries had an effect on both sides of the Atlantic. In particular, the Azores has developed a special relationship with the United States. More than half the population there have friends or relatives who live in the United States, and there are U.S. Air Force bases on the islands of Santa María and Terceira.

Immigrants who returned to the Azores helped Americanize the way of life there. Portuguese ethnographer Leite de Vasconcellos wrote that the returnees were transforming everything, from clothing and types of dwelling to language. She noted the presence of American furniture in many Azorean homes and English words in the Portuguese vocabulary. Azorean newspapers in the late 1930s reported that returnees introduced English expressions, modern farming methods, and Western clothing fashions. Another Azorean writer reported that "repatriates have brought into the Azores American ideas of liberty, mutual respect, regional autonomy, and interest in schools and literacy."

Portuguese immigrants arriving in Canada in 1957. Iberians have continued to immigrate to North America in the post–World War II era.

Immigration Continues

Although the largest waves of immigration from Iberia took place in the late 1800s and early 1900s, Portuguese, Spanish, and Basque settlers continue to come to North America. Today they are welcomed by well-established ethnic communities complete with social groups, churches, newspapers, and radio programs in their own language and special English-as-a-second-language classes in the schools.

Like the earlier groups of immigrants, the new arrivals seek out others from their homeland. However, in some cases the experience of the new immigrants is so different from that of those who came earlier that they form two distinct groups. José Luis Relinque, who emigrated from Spain in 1974 when he was 20, said he does not see many other Spaniards. Most of those he does meet are from the older generation and are much more conservative than he. Although he arrived with no money, he termed his emigration as more of an "adventure" than a quest for a better life. He arrived with plans to finish his college education but went to work instead, progressing from dishwasher to chef and restaurant owner. Rather than clinging to his Spanish background, he said he felt it important to become fluent in English and immerse himself in American culture so that he could find jobs more easily.

The immigrants of today come from a more prosperous Iberia than did their ancestors. Today's healthier economies offer them a greater variety of jobs, and they are generally better educated. Still, Spain and Portugal are among Europe's poorer nations, and in many cases America still offers more diverse opportunities than are available at home.

The Portuguese constitute the highest percentage of new arrivals of any group of European origin. Between 1971 and 1975, more than 52,000 Portuguese settled in the United States. So many went to New England that in 1974 the Rhode Island Department of Motor Vehicles published the first driver's manual ever issued in Portuguese in the United States.

The Iberians who have come to North America since World War II have been motivated by many reasons other than the simple economic incentives that drove their forefathers. Many are dissatisfied with the political

A Spanish-style Catholic church in the village of Villanueva, New Mexico. The Spanish influence on American culture is particularly evident in the Southwest.

leadership of their country and want to absent themselves from it. Others feel constrained by generations of tradition and seek a freer, more individual way of life. Still others seek a better education. And, like those who came before, a substantial number emigrate to join friends or relatives.

The Future for Iberian Americans

Many Iberian-American families today can count back five or more generations to the ancestors who immigrated to North America. Several generations removed from their immigrant forebears, they have been thoroughly assimilated and are likely to know about their kinsmen's experiences in the old country and their early years in the United States only through literature, family stories, and the activities of ethnic social clubs and heritage societies. Although their ties to America are much stronger than their faint connections to Spain or Portugal or the Basque country, they are proud of their heritage and the ethnic traditions that persist in their lives.

Among Iberian immigrants and their descendants, things have changed. Basques are no longer exclusively sheepherders, nor are the Portuguese and Spanish just mill workers or farmers. Today the Iberians and their children are becoming doctors, lawyers, and college professors and are entering many other professions. There are also still those who share their unique cultures through ethnic restaurants and stores or who continue to pursue a rural life much as they did back on the Iberian Peninsula, but for Iberian Americans, the range of opportunity available to them has never been broader. Each generation is a little better off economically, educationally, and in many other ways, and the community continues to be revitalized by the ongoing Iberian immigration. For these new arrivals, as for the descendants of those who came before them, America remains a land of infinite promise.

FURTHER READING

Adamic, Louis. *A Nation of Nations*. New York: Harper & Brothers Publishers, 1944.

Basch, H. "Basque Country, USA National Basque Festival in Elko, Nevada." *Travel Holiday*, July 1984.

Benton, Barbara. *Ellis Island, A Pictorial History*. New York: Facts on File , 1985.

Bilbao, Jon, and William A. Douglass. *Amerikanuak*. Reno: University of Nevada Press, 1975.

Brown, Francis J., and Joseph Roucekl. *One America*. Englewood Cliffs, NJ: Prentice-Hall, 1957.

Cardozo, Manoel da Silveira. *The Portuguese in America 590* B.C.–*1974*. Dobbs Ferry, NY: Oceana Publications, 1976.

Douglass, William A., and Beltran Paris. *Beltran, Basque Sheepman of the American West*. Reno: University of Nevada Press, 1979.

Gibson, Charles. *Spain in America*. New York: Harper & Row, 1966.

Laxalt, Robert. "Discovery in Labrador—16th-Century Basque Whaling Port." *National Geographic*, July 1985.

———. " The Indomitable Basques." *National Geographic*, July 1985.

Natella, Arthur A. *The Spanish in America, 1513–1979*. Dobbs Ferry, NY: Oceana Publications, 1980.

Ortega, Noel. *Spaniards in America*. Philadelphia, PA: Balch Institute, 1976. Pamphlet.

Pap, Leo. *The Portuguese Americans*. Boston, MA: G. K. Hall, 1981.

Rogers, Francis M. *Portuguese in America*. Philadelphia, PA: Balch Institute, 1974. Pamphlet.

Tavares, Belmira E. *Portuguese Pioneers in the United States*. Fall River, MA: R. E . Smith Printing Co., 1980.

Williams, Jerry. *And Yet They Come*. New York: Center for Migration Studies, 1982.

INDEX

PICTURE CREDITS

Alinari/Art Resource: pp. 32, 33; Architect of the Capitol Collection: pp. 12–13; Multicultural Section, Archives of Ontario: p. 105; Art Resource: p. 34; Bancroft Library: p. 18; The Bettmann Archive: pp. 96, 98; Bridgeman Art Library/Art Resource: p. 31; Theodore DeBry: p. 30; Jose Ortiz Echague/Art Resource: p. 41; Ferenz Fedor/Courtesy Museum of New Mexico (neg. no. 103534): p. 20; J. A. Freitas Library-U.P.E.C. Cultural Center: pp. 45, 48, 82; Courtesy of Andy Gavin. Photo from U.P.E.C Cultural Center: p. 55; Hawaii State Archives: pp. 65, 80; Hirmer Fotoarchive: p. 28; Richard Lane: pp. 22, 49, 68, 72; Richard Lane/Northeastern Nevada Museum: p. 83; Robert Laxalt Collection, Special Collections Department, University of Nevada-Reno Library: pp. 90–91; Library of Congress: pp. 14, 19, 21, 51, 52–53, 66, 73, 74–75, 78, 79; Buddy Mays: pp. 61 (top), 106; Courtesy of the Museum of New Mexico (neg. no. 37917): p. 17; Mark Nohl, New Mexico Economic and Tourism Department: p. 59 (bottom); Old Dartmouth Historical Society: pp. 23, 42–43, 44, 47; Oregon Historical Society: p. 67; Organization of American States: p. 24; Vernon Salvador: pp. 39, 84; Katrina Thomas: pp. 57, 58–59, 59 (top), 60–61, 61 (bottom), 62 (top, bottom), 63, 64, 102; UPI/Bettmann Newsphotos: pp. 35, 36, 37, 87, 93, 95, 100, 101

SUE FAGALDE LICK is a descendant of Iberian immigrants on both sides of the family. A lifelong resident of San Jose, California, she earned a degree in journalism from San Jose State University in 1974 and has been a newspaper reporter and editor for the past 15 years. She has also published short stories, poetry, and magazine articles.

DANIEL PATRICK MOYNIHAN is the senior United States senator from New York. He is also the only person in American history to serve in the cabinets or subcabinets of four successive presidents—Kennedy, Johnson, Nixon, and Ford. Formerly a professor of government at Harvard University, he has written and edited many books, including *Beyond the Melting Pot, Ethnicity: Theory and Experience* (both with Nathan Glazer), *Loyalties*, and *Family and Nation*.